The Writer's Guide to Authentic Dialogue Scenes

The Writer's Guide to Authentic Dialogue Scenes

Craft Vibrant Characters and Vivid Conversations

S. A. Soule

FWT

No part of this publication may be reproduced, stored in a retrieval system, or transmitted, in any form or by any means, without the prior permission in writing of the publisher, nor be otherwise circulated in any form of binding or cover other than that in which it is published and without a similar condition including this condition being imposed on the subsequent purchaser.

FBI Anti-Piracy Warning: The unauthorized reproduction or distribution of a copyrighted work is illegal. Criminal copyright infringement, including infringement without monetary gain, is investigated by the FBI and is punishable by up to five years in federal prison and a fine of $250,000.

The Writer's Guide to Dialogue
ISBN: 978-1530840526

Copyright © 2015 S. A. Soule.

Cover art by SwoonWorthy Book Covers

All rights reserved. Your support of the author's rights is appreciated.

Typesetting services by BOOKOW.COM

For Storytellers

Contents

INTRODUCTION	1
DIALOGUE TAGS	3
WRITING DIALOGUE	7
DUPLICATION	13
DIALOGUE SCENES	21
DIALOGUE PUNCTUATION	25
ENHANCE CONVERSATIONS	36
AUTHENTIC DIALOGUE	39
DEEP POV EXCHANGES	48
TALKING HEADS	53
INTERNAL EXPOSITION	59
CRAFTING GREAT DIALOGUE	64
INSERTING TENSION	72
INTENSIFYING CONFLICT	76
REALISTIC CONVERSATIONS	81
DIALOGUE DESCRIPTIONS	85
BONUS READING	89

CHARACTER EMOTION	90
DEEP POINT-of-VIEW METHOD	97
VIVID SETTINGS AND CHARACTERS	105
PLOTTING A NOVEL	112
HUMBLE REQUEST	118
FICTION WRITING TOOLS	119
ABOUT THE AUTHOR	128

INTRODUCTION

Dear Writer,

I've been writing most of my life, and even though I've studied the craft for years, I still love developing my skills as a writer, and I'm assuming that since you purchased this guide that you do, too.

First I thought I'd share a little about myself...I have over fifteen years of experience on all sides of the publishing business. I was a Creative Writing major in college, and I once owned an eBook publishing company where I edited hundreds of manuscripts. Then I worked as a developmental editor for another publisher, and in the last five years, I've even had the honor of editing books for a number of successful authors.

In the past, I've been traditionally published and also by a smaller indie publisher, and I've even self-published my work. Currently, I've written eleven fiction novels and eight nonfiction titles, but it wasn't until 2015 that I became a bestselling author, and the road to success has been a long journey. Many of my books have spent time on the 100 Kindle bestseller lists and some of my fiction has been chosen as top picks in the "Best Paranormal Romance" categories at several prominent review sites.

In this writing and self-editing guide, I share some of the wisdom that I've gleamed from various workshops and online courses over the years, along with the savvy advice from bestselling novelists and professional editors with whom I've had the pleasure to work with. This manual provides step-by-step instructions on ways to create realistic emotions, visceral responses, and powerful dialogue scenes that writers can easily and quickly apply to their own writing. Plus, I've included insightful and inspiring quotes as additional encouragement by popular writers and bloggers.

Writers should use the tips and tools covered in this guide as an arsenal of creative knowledge to include in their writer's toolbox. My goal is always for writers to come away with stronger writing and editing abilities that they can utilize in their own stories and give their audience a more personal reading experience.

There are a ton of great writing books and helpful blogs out there, so I hope my small contribution to the craft inspires you!

Happy writing and revising,

S. A. Soule

DIALOGUE TAGS

Quote: "Writing convincing dialogue is one of the hardest things for new writers to master. In fact, it's so rarely done well in any form of fiction that when it is done right, people rally around it. The movie Pulp Fiction, Terry McMillan's novel Waiting to Exhale, and the TV series My So-Called Life were all remarkable in large part because of how believably the characters spoke." —*Science Fiction writer, Robert J. Sawyer*

This first chapter covers basics such as how to use dialogue tags or beats correctly. As a professional developmental editor, I critique hundreds of manuscripts for fiction writers and dialogue seems the hardest for writers to write well. Personally, I use a software program that reads the text out loud for me. It's great to hear the rhythm and flow of your character interactions and the conversations to make sure the dialogue sounds natural. If you don't have access to a program, which can read your text for you—read it out loud to yourself. Or better yet, find someone to read it to you. It makes a *huge* difference in your dialogue.

Some of you might be wondering what the term "dialogue tag" means…

Well, "dialogue tags" are the additions to dialogue that identify the speaker. Without them, the reader would get confused as the conversations unfold, or if you have more than two characters speaking to each other within a scene. Readers need dialogue tags and saidisms that don't distract from the narrative. (Saidisms are just alternative words that mean "said" that are used to indicate additional information that is not expressed through the actual dialog or in the character description.)

Dialogue tags (also called by some writers and editors as saidisms or speech tags) are simple indications that allow the reader to identify each speaker. If there are only two characters in a scene, then it is not necessary to place a tag after each line of dialogue. Occasionally, you can use the character's unique speech patterns to distinguish which character is speaking.

Current writing style guidelines prefer that all dialogue tags identify the character first, and then the speech tag. It should be written as: "Nick said" instead of "said Nick." If you are self-publishing your work, these are the type of important writing techniques that you should keep in mind.

A good editing tool to remember is to avoid the overuse of adverbs that end in "ly." For example, "Max said mysteriously," or "Ashley said dryly" in the dialogue. Sure, a few are okay, but I suggest that writers try not to overdo it. These types of adverbs added onto the speech tags *tell* and don't *show*, which take a writer out of Deeper POV. Try to stick to using the general, "said / say" tags. The reader's eyes will simply pass over "said" and never even realize they've read it.

DIALOGUE TAGS

While acceptable, words such as "hollered" and "bawled" and "cried" often draw their attention away from the dialogue and yank your reader out of the story. So, in short, avoid saturating your dialogue scenes with tags such as: *cried, whispered, screeched, whined, declared, questioned, demanded, roared, hissed,* or *breathed.* These words appear as if you have become a little too chummy with your thesaurus. If the dialogue is well written, a few carefully placed tags like, "said/say" will often do just fine.

Also, try to avoid using too many descriptors like "yelled," or "said angrily," or "cried out," as a description of the character's emotion. The dialogue tag should allow the reader to interpret how something is being spoken without "telling" them. And remember that the word "said" is invisible to readers in dialogue text, while too many description tags can be off-putting to the reader.

While readers tend to read over the basic "said/say" tag, discernible attempts to insert a mixture of words such as "exclaimed," "shouted," or "teased," will completely pull the reader out of the narrative. If the writer has written skillful dialogue, then the reader is conscious that the character is exclaiming, bellowing, or mocking. The writer won't have to include it in the saidism.

How to write dialogue correctly:

Dialogue is set apart or identified with quotation marks. "Words spoken." To create realistic dialogue, it does not have to be written in complete sentences. In real life conversations, people don't always use proper grammar, either. So make certain that your dialogue sounds like what a person would actually say in a real conversation.

Each character needs their own individual voice.

Please make sure that all of your characters sound differently. They should not speak the same way or sound the same.

If you're writing a crime-drama, your vengeful, homicidal housewife should not sound the same as an alcoholic surgeon who just lost a patient on the operating table. Study current slang and modern trends. Give each character their own unique voice.

WRITING DIALOGUE

Quote: "Think about context. In this case, by "context" I mean your character's background and surroundings. A high-class 18th-century woman is going to speak very differently from an uneducated man of that time, or a teenager in today's society, or a king from another world. How your characters speak, what they choose to say and to whom is very much dependent on the setting, your character's background, and personality, which are all important to remember while writing dialogue." —*YA Sci-Fi and Fantasy novelist, Ava Jae*

Almost every scene that features dialogue should have tension, conflict, action, and emotion. If your stories are dialogue heavy, and there's marginal action, emotion, or description, try to revise the dialogue as much as possible—make it vivacious, intriguing, snarky, humorous, and concise. Don't give everyone a long monologue; let conversations unfold naturally. And don't forget to add tension, which can be sexual tension, passionate retorts, or intense arguments. Good dialogue should *always* reveal either characterization, backstory, or propel the story forward in some way.

It is important to realize that fictional dialogue should strive to capture and hold the reader's attention. If your characters ramble on, the way people do in real life, you'll lose your readers.

The best advice I can offer you?

Study dialogue written by your favorite authors diligently. Examine how they build suspense and structure a scene while the characters are speaking. Then apply it to your own writing. Observe how the writer broke up the dialogue or inserted a descriptive or action (gesture or body language) tag instead of a saidism to convey which character is talking. Avoid using too many "said / say" or "asked / ask" tags. And while revising your own scenes, remember to keep them from being stagnant and repetitive by using descriptive details and connecting the characters to the setting.

Up the tension, the emotion, and the action!

Try inserting action, emotion, or facial descriptions into the narrative. If an action or reaction is laced throughout the conversation, then the reader will get a vivid image of what is going on between the characters without being told. These important aspects can heighten any scene.

If you have a dialogue heavy scene, use this checklist. Ask yourself these questions:

Does the dialogue add tension or suspense to the current scene?

What are you trying to convey through this dialogue exchange?

Does the dialogue propel the plot forward?

Are the characters reactions realistic?

Are the characters connected to the setting by interacting within it?

Is it clear which character speaking in every line of dialogue?

Adding a few reactions, gestures, and descriptive tags within any dialogue scene will help your narrative become more powerful and real for the reader. People move when they talk, they use their hands, their facial expressions change while they're communicating, and they often gesture, point, move, and pace. Attempt to keep a story moving forward by mixing up description with the conversations, and even adding a character's emotional reactions into every dialogue scene.

This excerpt is from my paranormal romance novel, IMMORTAL ECLIPSE, and it is a great example of mixing description, character reactions, and emotion:

Walking up and down the beach, I take shots from interesting angles and a few that reflect the natural, timeless landscape. I lose track of time, caught up in the beautiful ripples running through the ocean.

"We have to stop meeting like this."

I turn, one hand flying to cover my pounding heart. "It's *you*."

The lighting is such that the deep blue of Dorian's T-shirt—a color he should wear all the time—makes his skin glow and his eyes glitter. He's so beautiful when he's smiling, and his laughing eyes are amazing.

He chuckles, an eruption of genuine laughter. But it sounds rusty, as if he hasn't laughed in a long time. He turns back to the trail before facing me again. A furrow of confusion wrinkles his brow. "Hey, how did you get here so quickly?"

"I went down the path."

"No, I mean, did you take a shortcut from the stables? And how did you change clothes so fast?"

"I'm a ninja?" I smile. "How fast is fast? I've been here for about an hour."

"That's impossible. I saw you," he says without a hint of doubt in his voice. "Sure, it was from a distance, but it *had* to be you."

"You're mistaken."

"You were standing outside the stables less than five minutes ago. So how did you get to the beach before me?"

"I don't know what to tell you. It wasn't me."

His eyebrows squish together and his eyes narrow to slits of glimmering blue. "Why are you lying?"

My eye twitches. I hate that feeling of being accused of lying when I'm actually not. I'd thrust a fist into his face—but I don't want to put my camera down near the sand. "I won't even try to answer that, it's so absurd. If you saw somebody near the stables, it wasn't *me*. Period."

We frown at each other.

He scratches his head. "There's no way it could have been anyone else."

This is so bizarre. What the hell is going on here? I'd been so busy focusing on other things that I haven't given this much thought until now.

"You know, this isn't the first time someone has mentioned that," I say. "First, this security guard from my old job swore he saw me in the office late one night. Then Emma claimed to have seen me in the dining room when I wasn't there, and Moesha swore she saw me in the library. And, Clayton accused me of carrying rope into the house the day Joshua died. Now you're insisting I was hanging out by the stables when I've been here the whole time."

After another terse silence, Dorian clears his throat. "That *is* really weird."

I shrug. "Maybe someone working here, one of the staff, looks similar to me."

He kicks at a rock, not meeting my eyes. "I don't think so."

***

As you can see from this excerpt, dialogue scenes can advance the story and amplify the character's personalities while providing a break from straight exposition.

Now I challenge you to try rewriting a dialogue scene in your own work-in-progress by including sensory details, reactions, and emotive responses.

DUPLICATION

Quote: "...*Rule 1: Dialogue Must Be In Conflict.* It's obvious, really. Just as a description of two young lovers spending a perfect day out at the zoo doesn't constitute a plot (not unless the girl falls in the lion enclosure!)... so two people chatting about nothing much at all (and not disagreeing with each other, either) doesn't constitute dialogue. Pleasant conversations are great in real life. Even if nothing especially interesting gets said, who doesn't like chewing the fat with a neighbor over the fence or a friend over coffee?

Listening in on those conversations, as a third party, would be about as exciting as watching laundry dry. So make sure you don't subject your readers to tedious, yawn-inducing dialogue in your novel.

How do you ramp up the excitement? Easy...

Give the two characters conflicting goals – one of them wants one thing, the other something else. Even if it doesn't end in a shouting match here and now, the underlying tension will be all you need to keep the readers turning those pages..." —*author and poet, Harvey Chapman, from the 9 Rules of Writing Dialogue*

To be honest, I do have a pet peeve about dialogue: *try not to duplicate yourself.* Avoid having your characters repeat back information. It is a sure sign of a newbie or amateur writer. And that's *not*—you! Right?

Bad example:

"Charlie, are you going downtown to the store later?" Marc asked.

"Yes, I'm going downtown to the store later," Charlie replied.

Good example:

Marc scratched his nose and asked, "Hey dude, you going to the store later, or what?"

"Yup. Gonna pick up some beer and snacks," Charlie replied, bobbing his head. "Hope the party doesn't suck."

Action example:

"You're late again, Katie!" Patricia looked at her watch. "How much time does it take to put on your shoes, anyway?"

Action example:

"Didn't anybody do the homework?" Miss Hall tapped her ruler on the desk. "There will be a test on this chapter tomorrow."

Be creative and use a descriptive or action tag instead.

It will make your scenes more realistic and visual for the reader. (Of course, writers shouldn't go crazy with action tags either) Also, don't have too many dialogue tags followed by an action.

DUPLICATION

Bad example:

"I'm going to the store. Be back soon." Noel yelled, grabbing her keys off the counter.

Good example:

Noel grabbed her keys off the counter and walked to the door. "I'm going to the store! Be back soon."

***

This next longer example was again taken from my novel, IMMORTAL ECLIPSE to show you how to properly use dialogue tags and punctuation. This excerpt will also show writers how to weave in action, description, tension, and a character's emotional reaction to enhance your scenes.

"Sky! Come in here." Pauletta's voice is so abrupt that I jump.

Damn. I just want to hide in my office, drink what's left of the mocha, and inspect yesterday's prints for *W* magazine.

I enter her spacious corner office with a fake smile plastered on my face. About time she realizes that I'm overdue for a promotion. She must be thrilled with the cover I did for *Glamour*. Maybe it didn't matter that I turned in my proofs a day late—it was some of my best work. Plus, I shot a beautiful fashion editorial for *Cosmopolitan*. Now I can take that vacation I've been putting off for the last three years and pay off those credit cards.

I'll get a bigger office with a view. *And* I'll be able to afford those Jimmy Choo ankle-boots I've being eyeing at Barneys.

My day has majorly improved.

"We need to talk," Pauletta says.

Behind her glass-top desk, she sits in a sleek black leather chair, which reclines to an almost obscene angle as she crosses her smooth brown legs. She's wearing a silk Hermès scarf draped over a gray blouse, with a matching rayon skirt, and a pair of *really* cute Bettye Muller heels. The open blinds allow placid sunlight to highlight the framed magazine covers and commercial advertisements lining the walls.

"I know I said I'd be in by ten, but I couldn't catch a cab—"

"It's fine." Pauletta shifts restlessly, her burgundy blazer rustling. "Skylar, how long have you worked for me?"

"Four years."

"That's right!" she exclaims, as if I've won a prize for guessing correctly, punctuating her words by jabbing a finger in the air. "We've worked together for a long time. I was the one who gave you your start in the business, and you've been my best employee. Until recently." Pauletta shakes her tight, black curls and then releases a long sigh.

Uh-oh. Where's she going with this? I'm standing near the desk, and my camera bag sits on the floor beside my feet. The urge

DUPLICATION

to grab it and run strikes hard and fast. Suddenly I have a bad feeling I'm in for a scolding.

"Even though we create beautiful images and call ourselves artists, this business is *still* a business." Pauletta clicks the top of her metal pen a few times. "Over the last six months, you've shown up late to photo shoots, missed deadlines, *and* don't even get me started on your attitude—"

"I've worked my ass off for this company!" My forced smile falters. I lift my chin, indignation coloring my tone. "Given up my social life, ignored holidays with friends, and even skipped vacations. I don't even date." Shifting my weight and trying to ignore the painful blister forming on my right pinky toe, I wipe sweaty palms on my ruined shirt. "Not to mention, I haven't had sex—"

"Whoa there!" Pauletta waves her hands.

Oh god, I am *so* oversharing. So much for female bonding.

"Look, I know you've made sacrifices," she says. "Who hasn't? And it's not like I don't appreciate your dedication, but let's be honest, your heart's not in it anymore, and that disinterest shows in your work." She blows out a breath. "My advice? Meet with the attorney you mentioned in San Francisco. Enjoy the California sunshine and fresh air."

Seriously? She's not promoting me. No raise. No corner office. And worse of all—no new boots.

***

Did that spark your creative muse? Here is one more.

This next excerpt was taken from a novel in my young adult series, MOONLIGHT MAYHEM, and it is a good example of showing tension in dialogue and adding a Deeper POV.

The fluorescent lamps gleamed on Trent's pale hair. "Hey, guys."

"Hi, Trent," Ariana said.

He smiled at Ari, and then faced me again. "How you doing, Shiloh?"

He stared at me as if Ari wasn't sitting there watching. My ears stung hot and my neck flushed. Nerves snapped and jumped beneath my skin.

"I've been okay," I said, and fiddled with my straw. Heat flared on my skin at his nearness.

Music blasted from the speakers, the singer doing a rendering of *Linkin Park's* "In The End" that pulsated through me. Trent's eyes roamed over my body, then my lips. My face burned even hotter from his long stare. I crossed and uncrossed my legs.

Ariana raised one thin brow in Trent's direction. "Who are you here with?"

"My buddy Lance. He's over there." He pointed to the J. Crew catalog-looking boy standing beside the register. "We're planning to grab a pizza and head back to my place to play X-Box."

I took a sip from my glass of diet soda, careful not to let liquid dribble on my chin.

"Uh, Shiloh, just thought I'd let you know that I'm transferring schools next quarter," Trent announced. "We'll be at Redwood High together."

Soda squirted from my mouth and sprayed the table. "W-what?"

Ariana smacked me on the back while I choked and sputtered. "Why switch schools at the beginning of your senior year?" she asked.

"Tired of driving into the city every day." Trent grabbed a napkin and wiped the table. One side of his lip curled into a half-smile. He jerked his chin at me. "She gonna be okay?"

"Yup. Just went down the wrong pipe," Ari answered for me.

Soon we would be attending the same school. Not sure how I felt about that.

Trent's eyes locked on mine. "What've you been up to since my party?"

Small talk? Really?

I wiped my mouth and pushed the soda away before responding. "Um, you know, just hanging out." I played with my straw, avoiding eye contact.

Ugh, how lame did that sound? Obviously, we were just hanging out.

"You guys wanna join us—*ouch!*" Ariana did her best to hide the pain from my sharp kick under the table. She sweetly smiled at Trent. "Another time, perhaps?"

He gave me a sidelong glance. His stare fierce, edged in shadow. "Sure. Another time."

***

Well-written dialogue propels the plot forward and fleshes out the characters motives and personalities. However, just as realistic dialogue is one of the most powerful tools at a writer's disposal. It takes time to develop a good ear.

Always try to show. Use Deep POV. Don't rely on tags to convey emotion. Edit out the filler words and unessential dialogue — that is, the dialogue that doesn't contribute to the plot in some way.

DIALOGUE SCENES

Quote: "Perhaps it's a lack of confidence on the writer's part, perhaps its simple laziness, or perhaps it's a misguided attempt to break up the monotony of using "said" all the time, but all too many fiction writers tend to pepper their dialogue with *ly* adverbs…" —*Renni Browne and Dave King, from Self-Editing For Fiction Writers*

The Deep POV method is an amazing tool that can immediately turn a writer's dialogue into stronger, more emotive scenes. This is frequently a difficult skill to master for some writers, but it's so effective that it will amplify any scene within a manuscript. Deep POV can put the reader so firmly into the character's head that the writer basically vanishes.

One of the best ways to avoid *telling* in your writing is through dialogue, which can help deepen characterization, reveal emotions, and even accentuate mood and theme. Reading an engaging dialogue scene makes a reader feel as if they're actually eavesdropping on a real conversation.

What disappears in a Deeper POV dialogue scene are the need for lots of intrusive dialogue tags with the "ly" adverbs (emotional qualifiers) attached to them, which are the John said angrily, Jane asked sadly, Max said irritably.

Dialogue tags used as emotional qualifiers like yelled, said crossly, or cried out, as a description of the character's emotional state can often cause author intrusion. Author intrusion is only one drawback with using "ly" adverbs in our dialogue because it also tacks on an emotional qualifier that often creates shallower writing.

So try to avoid the overuse of emotional qualifiers in conversations. A few are okay, but don't overdo it because these types of tags *tell* and don't *show*, which takes a writer out of Deeper POV.

(In the shallow examples, I have underlined what I consider shallower writing (telling) and obtrusive "ly" adverbs.) Please examine these sentences…

SHALLOW: "Do you know where the treasure is hidden?" she asked anxiously.

DEEP POV: She clenched her jaw. "Do you know where the treasure is hidden or not?"

SHALLOW: "This is private property and you're trespassing," I yelled coldly.

DEEP POV: I crossed both arms over my chest. "This is private property and *you're* trespassing."

DIALOGUE SCENES

SHALLOW: "Charles never takes me anywhere fun," she <u>said bitterly</u>.

DEEP POV: Clenching her teeth, she muttered, "Charles *never* takes me anywhere fun."

The dialogue tag should allow the reader to know who spoke without *telling* them the emotion behind the words. Most "ly adverbs" can be revised by using Deeper POV, which will give your dialogue scenes greater impact. Learn to be ruthless and omit those emotional qualifiers.

(In the shallow examples, I have underlined what I consider shallower writing (telling) and those annoying "ly" adverbs.) Please compare these next sentences...

SHALLOW: "Give it back," Amber <u>shouted threateningly</u>.

DEEP POV: "Give it back!" Amber's hard stare bore into me like two heat seeking missiles.

SHALLOW: "Please don't hurt me," Thomas <u>pleaded miserably</u>.

DEEP POV: Thomas recoiled and his voice sounded weak. "*Please* don't hurt me."

SHALLOW: "Don't be such a jerk," Samson <u>said scornfully</u>.

DEEP POV: "Don't be such a jerk," Samson said through gritted teeth.

SHALLOW: "Stay back!" he <u>yelled loudly in anger</u>. "Or else."

DEEP POV: "Stay back!" His voice rose and his body tensed. "Or else."

If writers use other types of tags like *roared, implored, wailed, hollered, suggested, noted, remarked, answered, begged, crooned,* or *complained,* it will almost certainly take them out of Deep POV and be distracting to the reader.

To use a Deeper POV in your dialogue scenes, writers should try not to use dialogue tags other than "said" or "asked" most of the time. These tags are invisible to the reader, yet they let the reader know which character is speaking. Some editors state that it is redundant for a writer to use *asked* after a question mark, but I think it is fine if needed to identify the speaker.

Now I encourage writers to study how to properly use a combo of action tags, emotional responses, and dialogue tags in their conversations.

DIALOGUE PUNCTUATION

Quote: "…If you have a character with a strong accent, you might be tempted to indicate this in every line of dialogue they speak. Tread very lightly here. If you're peppering your character's speech with apostrophes and creative spellings, it's going to make the reader's life hard. It can also give the inadvertent and unfortunate impression that you're looking down on or even mocking that character's region, class background, or race. Instead of writing words out phonetically, try using occasional dialect words, or unusual word order, to indicate a character's speech patterns…" —*author, Joanna Penn, of The Creative Penn*

If within the dialogue, it seems unclear or vague which character is doing the talking, then it is important to always add a tag to reveal the character. A tag can be placed in the middle of the dialogue or after the dialogue with a simple speech tag.

It is not always necessary to identify which character is speaking with a dialogue tag, if there are only two characters talking in a scene. In dialogue, where a character is identified by an action, then writers can skip including a dialogue tag, too. No need for both.

Dialogue Example:

Sammy grunts. "Mom, do I need to eat all of my veggies?" His voice rises in a whiny pitch.

His mother sighs wearily. "Yes, sweetheart. I had to when I was a kid. Just ask your grandpa."

"Is that true?" Sammy shifts in his seat to face the older man sitting across from him. "Did she have to eat this icky stuff when she was a kid?" He pokes at the green beans on his plate with a fork.

Grandpa reaches across the table to pat his grandson's hand. "Of course. Now eat up, kiddo."

***

As a rule, each time a different character speaks, it should be in a new paragraph. This helps the reader know that the dialogue has changed from one character to another in the conversation. On occasion, a character's dialogue continues from one paragraph to a second paragraph. This is distinguished by not adding a closing quotation mark at the end of the first dialogue paragraph.

Think of dialogue paragraphs as that speaker "owning" that paragraph, and remember that the POV character's thoughts or actions should *never* invade another character's dialogue. Writers should always create a new paragraph to do that.

DIALOGUE PUNCTUATION

Here is an example taken from my vampire romance novella, FORBIDDEN NIGHT that is free to read on Wattpad. The sections that are underlined are introspection that invades another characters dialogue. Since the scene is written in Siobhan's POV, her thoughts should not be included within the other character's speech.

Incorrect Dialogue Example:

<u>Siobhan remained still, but she didn't answer. Her shoulders slumped.</u> Draven grinned. "Caleb is a fool. He hates being a vampire. He loathes our kind. I can see it in your violet eyes—*you crave darkness*—power. Like me. Besides, you've only know each other a few months. And he wasn't very honest with you, remember? But now that you've discovered our secret…" He tilted his head, listening to the night. His expression appeared thoughtful. "It doesn't matter. We can discuss this later—"

"Or we can talk about it *now*. Stop giving me the brush off." She straightened her posture. "You could say it was a shock at first—discovering you were vampires. But it's not as if I couldn't guess. I mean, you guys only show up after sunset, never eat, are extremely pale, and your eyes…sometimes they turn black." She sighed and a flush heated her cheeks. "I've read *Twilight* and *The Vampire Diaries*. Although I have to admit, I'm kinda disappointed that you guys don't sparkle."

Draven chuckled. <u>She thought that he never took her seriously, which was so frustrating. Why wouldn't Draven be serious for once?</u> "Sorry to disillusion you. But real vampires don't glow in the sunlight—they just burn to ash. Now you should really go back to bed." Draven moved inhumanly fast. One second he was five feet away, and the next he was beside her. <u>He looked frightening and her heart pounded hard.</u> "But not before I kiss you goodnight."

Correct Dialogue Example:

Siobhan remained still, but she didn't answer. Her shoulders slumped.

Draven grinned, flashing his sharp fangs. "Caleb is a fool. He hates being a vampire. He loathes our kind. I can see it in your violet eyes—*you crave darkness*—power. Like me. Besides, you've only know each other a few months. And he wasn't very honest with you, remember? But now that you've discovered our secret…" He froze, tilting his head and listening to the night. His expression tightened, his eyes narrowing on the trees. "It doesn't matter. We can discuss this later—"

"Or we can talk about it *now*. Stop giving me the brush off." Siobhan stepped closer, standing tall. "You could say it was a shock at first—discovering you were vampires. But it's not as if I couldn't guess. I mean, you guys only show up after sunset, never eat, are extremely pale, and your eyes…sometimes they turn black." She sighed and a flush heated her cheeks. "I've read *Twilight* and *The Vampire Diaries*. Although I have to admit, I'm kinda disappointed that you guys don't sparkle. "

Draven chuckled. "Sorry to disillusion you. But real vampires don't glow in the sunlight—they just burn to ash. Now you should really go back to bed."

DIALOGUE PUNCTUATION

Draven moved inhumanly fast. One second he was five feet away, and the next he was beside her. He was beyond frustrating and now he was in her personal space. His expression darkened and her heart beat wildly in her chest.

He lowered his head, his mouth inches from hers. "But not before I kiss you goodnight."

***

Writers should always indent each new section of dialogue, and double-check the punctuation and capitalization within the dialogue or action tags. Here are some examples of correct punctuation.

Always place a comma after the dialogue tag:

Jake said, "I am delighted."

Always place a comma before the dialogue tag:

"I am delighted," Jake said.

If a dialogue tag is in the middle of a character's speech, the first word after the tag is not capitalized unless the proper noun or personal pronoun requires it:

"Beyond that," she said, "who knows?"

"Even if you get to the treasure first," she said, "Jake won't."

If the end punctuation is an exclamation point or a question mark, the following word in the tag is still not capitalized:

"I am joyful!" Jake said.

Note the proper capitalization. If the dialogue tag follows the closed quote of the dialogue, the next word is capitalized if it is a proper noun, such as a name:

"I am blissful," Jake said.

When using action to identify the source of dialogue, each sentence stands alone with its punctuation:

Jake bounced on his heels. "I am delighted!"

Watch your comma use when adding action or information to a dialogue tag:

"I am fortunate," said Jake, his fist pumping the air.

"I am stoked," said Jake as his fist punching the air.

Question marks and asked tags are not always necessary.

Example with dialogue tag: "What do you expect to happen now?" Bradley asked.

Example without the speech tag, but with an action instead: Bradley tapped a finger on his chin. "What do you expect to happen now?"

First, given the author's use of a question mark, is it truly necessary to add that *he asked*? This is, in my opinion, one of the most overused and frustrating dialogue tags.

DIALOGUE PUNCTUATION

– Search for the dialogue tag words in the following list. Are you telling rather than showing? Do you absolutely need these words to get your meaning across, or is there another way you could show the meaning? Rewrite so that you only need to use *said, asked, whispered, yelled,* or the adverb examples discussed in this chapter.

If writers use any of the saidisms (speech tags) listed below within their dialogue, then I encourage authors to rewrite the dialogue so the shallow "telling" dialogue tag isn't needed.

List of words to cut from the dialogue:

acknowledged

admitted

agreed

answered

cut in

argued

babbled

barked

begged

bellowed

bemoaned (This is not considered a correct dialogue tag.)

breathed (This is not considered a correct dialogue tag.)

commented

complained

confessed

cried

croaked

crooned

crowed

demanded

denied (This is not considered a correct dialogue tag.)

drawled

echoed

faltered

fumed

giggled (This is not considered a correct dialogue tag.)

groaned (This is not considered a correct dialogue tag.)

growled

grumbled

DIALOGUE PUNCTUATION

heckled (This is not considered a correct dialogue tag.)

hinted

hissed (This is not considered a correct dialogue tag.)

howled (This is not considered a correct dialogue tag.)

implored (This is not considered a correct dialogue tag.)

inquired

inserted (This is not considered a correct dialogue tag.)

interjected

jested (This is not considered a correct dialogue tag.)

laughed (This is not considered a correct dialogue tag.)

nagged

offered

pleaded

pouted (This is not considered a correct dialogue tag.)

promised

queried (This is not considered a correct dialogue tag.)

questioned (This is not considered a correct dialogue tag.)

quipped

quoted

raged (This is not considered a correct dialogue tag.)

ranted

reiterated (This is not considered a correct dialogue tag.)

remembered (This is not considered a correct dialogue tag.)

requested

retorted

roared

ruminated (This is not considered a correct dialogue tag.)

scolded

screamed

screeched

shrieked

sighed (This is not considered a correct dialogue tag.)

snarled

snickered (This is not considered a correct dialogue tag.)

snorted (This is not considered a correct dialogue tag.)

sneered (This is not considered a correct dialogue tag.)

sobbed (This is not considered a correct dialogue tag.)

sputtered

stammered

stuttered

threatened

thundered

told

wailed

warned

whimpered

wondered (This is not considered a correct dialogue tag.)

yelped (This is not considered a correct dialogue tag.)

***

I encourage writers while doing revisions on their dialogue heavy scenes to use these suggestions and tools to enhance their own stories.

ENHANCE CONVERSATIONS

Quote: "Dialogue in fiction has five functions. One or more of the following must always be at work, or you're just taking up space on the page: 1) Reveal story information. 2) Reveal character. 3) Set the tone. 4) Set the scene. 5) Reveal theme…"
—*bestselling author, James Scott Bell*

One of the best ways to *show* is through dialogue, which is usually the most interesting aspect of fiction for any reader. But so often, writers don't create engaging dialogue scenes that arouse the reader's attention.

Most writers have heard or been told that the use of adverbs is considered a major writing offense because it is often a way of *telling* rather than *showing*.

In dialogue heavy scenes, writers need fresh ways to describe emotions directly to the reader instead of just "stating the feeling," which causes the dreaded *narrative distance* that I talked about in each book of the Fiction Writing Tools series.

The examples below are ones frequently found in fiction that will demonstrate why it is better not to *state the emotion* in dialogue tags.

ENHANCE CONVERSATIONS

(In the shallow examples, I have underlined what I consider shallower writing (telling) and obtrusive "ly" adverbs.) Please carefully compare these sentences…

SHALLOW: "I don't want to go to the dance this Friday night, Lucas!" I said <u>with frustration</u>.

DEEP POV: I threw my hands up and sighed. "For the hundredth time, Lucas, I *don't* want to go to that stupid dance on Friday."

SHALLOW: "Come here," he <u>said menacingly</u>.

DEEP POV: When he spoke, his tone was low and hard. "Come here. *Now*."

SHALLOW: "My puppy ran away and I can't find him," I <u>said sadly</u>.

DEEP POV: Tears clouded my vision. "My puppy ran away and I can't find him," I said, my voice cracking on the words.

SHALLOW: "Stop harassing my girlfriend," he <u>said angrily</u>.

DEEP POV: His hands formed fists at his sides. "You'd better *stop* harassing my girlfriend."

SHALLOW: "Get away from me!" I <u>shouted boisterously</u>.

DEEP POV: "Get away from me!" My voice sounded high and shrill.

SHALLOW: "Never enter my room without permission," she <u>demanded hotly</u>.

DEEP POV: Her expression turned cold and unyielding. *"Never enter my room without permission."*

SHALLOW: "Where were you between the hours of six and seven o'clock last night?" I <u>asked suspiciously</u>.

DEEP POV: I eyed him closely. "So, where were you between the hours of six and seven last night, huh?"

Those examples illustrated how writers can eliminate the "ly adverb" from their dialogue and express the emotion instead by *showing* and not *telling* to strengthen the scene. It is okay to use an adverb occasionally, but I suggest writers use them with caution and only rarely if needed.

AUTHENTIC DIALOGUE

Quote: "Create separate dialogue files for each character. More than anything else, a character's dialogue needs to sound consistent (unless, of course, you're using it to indicate character changes). By creating separate files, I can read straight through just what a character says and edit, then put it back into the novel." —*Darcy Pattison, storyteller, teacher, and founder of Mims House publisher*

I advise the writers that I work with to insert visual descriptions of facial expressions, body language, and gestures to convey emotions and reactions within the dialogue to make it come alive for the reader. (Writers can find amazingly helpful examples in my three bestselling guidebooks, "The Writer's Guide to Character Emotion," "The Writer's Guide to Character Emotion," and "The Writer's Guide to Vivid Settings and Characters" in the `FictionWritingTools` series on sale now in eBook, paperback, and audiobook formats.)

(In the shallow examples, I have underlined what I consider shallower writing (telling).) Please carefully examine this scene ...

SHALLOW:

My best friend Candace <u>looked furious</u> as she walked over to me. She expressed that she was <u>angry</u> because I had told her crush that she liked him. I <u>felt really bad</u>. I <u>saw</u> a crowd of girls gathered around us to <u>watch</u> the fight. Then I was <u>scared</u> that this misunderstanding would get out of hand. I did not know how to fix this, <u>I thought</u>.

DEEP POV (no dialogue tags):

Candace marched over to me with her nostrils flared. "I'm going to kill you! How *could* you tell Devin that I had a crush on him?"

Oops! I took a step back. "I'm sorry—"

"Save it." Candace rolled up the sleeves of her purple hoodie.

Several of our classmates made a tight circle around us as if waiting for an epic showdown. My best friend lifted her hands, curing her fingers into claws.

A girl from my Bio class shoved me from behind. "Cat fight!"

My heart rate tripled. I had to figure out a way out of this mess —and *fast!*

***

AUTHENTIC DIALOGUE

Some writers depend on the same one or two descriptors or adverbs to repeatedly describe an emotion or expression, but I encourage you to be creative and find fresh and unique ways to describe them.

This first scene has too many "emotional qualifiers" and the speech reads too formal. The scene also causes too much narrative distance with so many dialogue tags and "ly adverbs" that it will jolt the reader from the story.

(In the shallow examples, I have underlined what I consider shallower writing (telling), obtrusive "ly" adverbs, and clichéd writing.) Please carefully examine these longer scenes…

SHALLOW:

"Get ready!" Lucas shouted vociferously as he ran into the house in a big panic. "They are coming."

Ava looked up in surprise from her seat on the sofa. "Is it the vampires?" she asked intensely.

Lucas looked at his friends and his face was white with terror. "Yes. They have found our hideout!" he yelled vehemently.

"How many are there?" Oliver asked fearfully.

"There are twelve vampires," Lucas answered nervously.

"Did you see the vampire slayer, too?" Oliver asked impatiently.

Lucas looked thoughtful. "No. But I do hope that she is on her way," he answered pensively.

***

*Note: In all of the Deeper POV revised examples, I rewrite the shallower illustration to combine both "character voice" in the dialogue speech and in the characterization. If writers want to learn how to enhance a scene by deepening the POV, please study the other guidebooks in this series.

DEEP POV (only 1 dialogue tag):

The front door burst open and Lucas raced into the house. "Get ready!" His eyes were wild and he was breathing heavily. "*They're coming.*"

Ava jumped up from her seat and placed a hand over her thumping heart. "Is it the vampires?"

Lucas nodded, his face bleached of color. "Yes. They must've found our hideout."

"How many?" Oliver asked, his voice slightly trembling.

Lucas wrung his hands. "Twelve nasty blood suckers."

Oliver nodded. "Did you see the vampire slayer, too?"

Lucas scratched his head. "Um, no. But let's hope that she's on her way."

***

The second version is rewritten in Deep POV and is much more engaging to read. It *shows* the emotions and has more "character voice" in the narrative.

(In the shallow examples, I have underlined what I consider shallower writing (telling) and obtrusive "ly" adverbs.) Please carefully study this next scene…

SHALLOW:

"I saw your ex-boyfriend today," Mandy <u>said with concern</u>. "He said that he missed you."

"I do not accept that as true," I <u>said in surprise</u>. "Because it is hard to believe that when he broke up with me on Valentine's Day," I <u>said bitterly</u>.

DEEP POV:

"I ran into your ex…" My best friend gently rubbed my arm. "He even had the nerve to say that he missed you."

"*Seriously,* Mandy?" Shaking my head, I bitterly laughed. "That's hard to believe since the jerk dumped me on Valentine's Day."

***

Now this much longer scene is crammed with too many distracting dialogue tags that cause major author intrusion.

(In the shallow example, I have underlined what I consider shallower writing (telling) and obtrusive "ly" adverbs.) Please carefully study this extended scene…

SHALLOW:

Mia went over to the Thompson's house and she was <u>very distressed</u> when she arrived and went into the kitchen where she <u>saw</u> her friends.

"I know Eddie is cheating on me!" Mia <u>declared loudly</u>. "I saw him at *her* house today."

"Maybe he was just driving through the neighborhood," Isabella <u>suggested</u>.

"Sure," Logan <u>agreed</u>. "Ed is a good guy and he wouldn't be having an affair."

"I followed him from the office and he drove over there, and then he parked on her street," Mia <u>insisted</u>. Then she drank some wine that was on the counter. "He's definitely having an affair. I mean, face it," she <u>observed</u>. "Eddie is handsome and an influential doctor, and I have gained a lot of weight and gotten so flabby. So I know he is having an affair," she <u>claimed sadly</u>.

"You don't know that for sure," Logan <u>responded sympathetically</u>.

"He might have been going by the nanny's house to visit the kids," Isabella <u>offered</u>. "Mia, you said that sometimes the nanny takes the children back to her place."

"Maybe…but he did mention that he was going to be in a meeting all afternoon when I called this morning," Logan <u>confessed sheepishly</u>.

"It must be true. He is even lying to his friends. Now I am going over there to confront him," Mia <u>announced</u>.

Then her friends <u>watched</u> as she lifted her purse, and reached inside, and then she removed a handgun.

Now please compare this revised version with character "character voice," Deep POV, and sensory details added…

DEEP POV:

Mia marched through the Thompson's house and entered the bright yellow kitchen. She tossed aside her leather handbag and slumped onto a stool. "I know Eddie is cheating on me!" Tears clouded her blue eyes. "I caught the lying jerk at *her* house today."

Her best friends, Isabella and Logan, had been happily married for ten years. Both slim and blond, they looked like the perfect couple.

Isabella frowned, holding a bottle of wine in one hand. "Well, maybe he was just driving through the neighborhood." She poured the liquor into her crystal wineglass.

"That has to be why." Logan nodded, leaning his elbows against the counter. "Ed is a good guy and I doubt that he's having an affair."

"I followed him from the office and he drove straight over to her house." Mia sniffled and snatched a glass of wine off the counter, gulping the burgundy liquid down. "He's *definitely* having an affair. I mean, let's face it," she said, taking another sip of wine, this time from Logan's half-full glass. "Eddie is totally hot, and I've gained twenty pounds over the last year. Now I've got varicose veins and a flabby butt. Of course he's having an affair!"

Logan grunted. "You don't know that for sure."

"He might've been going by her house to visit the kids," Isabella said, her voice thick with sympathy. "Mia, you've mentioned that sometimes the nanny takes the children back to her place."

Logan fiddled with the wine bottle and avoiding Mia's stare. "Maybe…but Eddie told me that he was going to be in a meeting all afternoon when I called this morning."

Mia shook her head and fresh tears lined her eyes. The idea of her muscular-tanned-golf-loving husband having sex, let alone in the middle of the afternoon, with the skinny-designer-knock-off-wearing nanny made her want to rip the hair from her own head.

"*See!* He's even lying to his friends! I'm going over there to confront him." Mia squared her shoulders, then removed a handgun from her purse.

***

Which scene did you find more exciting and interesting?

The revised scene in Deeper POV with the added details makes the example much more dramatic and engaging. Those last two

AUTHENTIC DIALOGUE

examples demonstrate how writers can revise any heavy dialogue scenes with a Deeper POV to make them more intimate for their readers. When writers stay in close-and-personal with their audience, it can easily enhance the dialogue.

DEEP POV EXCHANGES

Quote: "Dialogue has only two purposes: (1) to enhance the characterization, and (2) to further the plot." —*Othello Bach*

Writing realistic dialogue does not come easily to everyone. Well-written dialogue advances the story while providing a respite from lengthy sections of introspection and it also helps to avoid author intrusion.

In James Scott Bell's guidebook (which I highly recommend reading), "*How to Write Dazzling Dialogue,*" he advises this for any novel:

1. Make a list of your cast. Give each character a one or two line description.

2. Step back and make sure the descriptions are sufficiently different from each other.

3. Give each character one quirk. Make them irritating to at least two other characters.

4. Write a few "practice scenes" pairing two of the characters together at random.

DEEP POV EXCHANGES

***

Another way to make dialogue more powerful is to include character "tics" or gestures throughout. Try to make sure that the characters have the correct responses and that they're reactions are clearly shown, but never outright stated to the reader.

Here are a few quick tips to revise dialogue and connect the conversation with the setting, senses, and Deeper POV.

1) Briefly describe the setting at the start of each new scene, such as an urban city, a coffee shop, a desolate farm, a graveyard, a dark forest, a high school bathroom. (Try to make the setting as vivid and visual as possible for your readers to avoid "talking heads" in a dialogue heavy scene. And mention the setting at least twice to remind the reader where the characters are between the speech.)

2) Give the characters moving body parts as they speak. (Real people are not statues when they're speaking. They gesture, grunt, cough, make faces, scratch, nod, shrug, etc.)

3) Show reactions through facial expressions and gestures. (When another character says something significant, the POV character should *show* a reaction. They can grimace, wince, shrug their shoulders, laugh, or blush, etc.)

4) Share the character's internal-thoughts. (In-between a dialogue exchange, share with the reader what the POV character is thinking internally. Have it conflict with what they say to really spice up the scene.)

5) Weave some connections to the setting and any objects by having characters interact with them. (Make sure that the characters interact with the environment, and also mention details, like a cold breeze, a howling dog, cars rushing past, the touch of cool metal, etc.)

6) Include the five senses: *what are the characters seeing, hearing, smelling, touching, etc.?* (Use the Deep POV method to make the scene come alive for your readers.)

7) Add a flourish of color. Mention the shade of the car, the paint on the walls, the color of the trees, etc. (Dialogue is not just about what the characters say, but it should also be connected to the setting so the characters are not floating around in space.)

***

Dialogue is a place where "character voice" is vital to revealing personality and character traits, along with making your characters seem more multi-dimensional. Weave a character's inner-thoughts and emotions into the narrative, and you'll notice an immediate difference.

This next excerpt was taken from my new adult novel, SMASH INTO YOU, and gives another example on how to incorporate Deep POV by including "character voice" sensory details, and description into the dialogue exchange.

Please closely examine this scene…

DEEP POV:

When the stranger stopped beneath the lamppost, the stream of incandescent light struck his body and shone on a head of unruly waves. He stood with his thumbs hooked into the loops of his jeans, with the strap of a backpack drooping from one broad shoulder. I caught the glint of a silver ring piercing his left eyebrow.

Fan-friggin'-tastic. I was alone in the quad with a dangerous-looking, pierced stranger. One who probably carried around a backpack full of paraphernalia used to torture innocent young women.

"You okay?" He took a step toward me. "You look kinda spooked—"

"Stop!" I aimed the pepper spray at him, holding one finger on the trigger. "Give me an extremely good reason not to blast you right now."

His hands went up in surrender. "*Whoa!* Don't shoot." He gazed steadily at me, his eyes bright under the streetlight. "I'm a student here, just waiting for someone."

Okay. So, it wasn't an insane-asylum escapee or a bloodthirsty murderer. Only another college student. The tension in my shoulders unwound, along with the muscles in the back of my neck.

He transferred the backpack from one shoulder to the other. "Sorry. I didn't mean to scare you."

My attempt at a smile felt forced. "And *I* didn't mean to almost blind you." I lowered my arm, but kept a wary eye on the guy.

***

There are no dialogue tags in that entire excerpt, but it is made clear which character is speaking and that the emotions are "shown" rather than "told" by what the first-person narrator is seeing, feeling, and interpreting.

It's very important for readers to be able to visibly imagine a character's facial expressions or reactions in a scene. In some dialogue scenes, a writer might need to *dig deeper* to describe emotional reactions and responses through body language and internal-thoughts without always having to use emotional qualifiers or adverbs.

TALKING HEADS

Quote: "Unless a dialogue exchange is grounded in a physical place, and I can see the physical bodies doing the speaking, what we have on the page are two talking heads." —*author and editor, Ramona DeFelice Long*

I love reading dialogue. Dialogue done correctly can quicken the pace of any novel, reveal characterization, add tension, or reveal the motives and/or goals of the characters. It can show two characters exchanging in witty banter, falling in love, or even add a dash of conflict and intrigue into a scene without *telling* the reader what's happening.

First, I'd like to discuss what some professional editors refer to as "talking heads" in dialogue heavy scenes. The term refers to any dialogue where it reads as if two or more heads are just floating around in space without any real connection to the setting or the scene itself. To correct this, writers should try adding in some sensory details (like the five senses), Deep POV, and action beats, which can substitute for a dialogue tag, as well as some internal-monologue.

The first scene has very stiff, almost formal speech, and there is no connection to the setting, nor does it reveal any insight into the characterization, and it has too many dialogue tags.

Please carefully compare these two scenes…

EXAMPLE of "TALKING HEADS":

"How long have you and Amanda been in a relationship? A long time?" Brenden asked.

"Yes, we have," Nick replied. "Why do you ask?"

"Did you sleep with her yet?"

"Do you mean have sex? No," Nick answered. "But I think we have only been dating for a few months."

"My girlfriend wants to wait to have sex, Brenden said. "Nonetheless, I would like to do it right away."

"It might be too soon to have sexual intercourse," Nick responded.

"I disagree," Brenden told Nick. "We have been dating for a very long time."

"Then why do you not just ask her why she wants to wait?" Nick questioned.

"I am fearful of scaring her off…because I love her," Brenden confessed.

"That is very good to hear, Brenden," Nick said. "Now can we please finish our lunch and not discuss our girlfriends?"

TALKING HEADS

***

In the first scene above, the reader has no idea where this conversation is taking place, what the characters are feeling, thinking, or their reactions.

Anytime dialogue is placed on its own, it creates a lot of narrative distance and even reader confusion. Readers can't visualize, or experience, or know what the characters are thinking, or even where the scene takes place. Readers become distanced from the story-world when there's no connection to the setting or visual interactions.

The next passage has been revised to incorporate sensory details, Deep POV, and "character voice" to enhance the scene and provide a clear visualize for the reader.

REVISED EXAMPLE:

The Chinese restaurant was quiet with only a few patrons. Rain pattered against the front window, beating out a dull symphony of taps. Nick sighed. The grey weather seemed to match his somber mood. A tall waitress wearing a stained apron came by the table to take their order, then scurried off.

Brenden leaned back in the leather booth. "You and Amanda have been going out a long time, right?"

Nick raised an eyebrow, but didn't reply. When Brenden had sent him text about meeting up for lunch, Nick had *not* expected a chat about relationships.

"Well?"

"Yes," Nick said, twisting his napkin around one finger. "Why?"

Brenden took a swig of his beer and set the bottle on the table with a clank. "You sleep with her yet?"

"Have sex? Not yet." Nick squirmed in his seat and the napkin in his hands tore in half. "But we've only been going out officially for like, three months." He slouched and his untouched glass of iced tea sweated on the crumb-coated tabletop. The tangy scent of fried onions and spicy foods flowed from the kitchen doorway and made Nick's stomach grumble.

"That's a really long time, dude. My girlfriend keeps telling me that we need to wait." Brenden grunted and reached for his beer again. "But, dude, if I had my way, we'd be doing it right now!"

This conversation was becoming way too chick-flick for Nick. The food couldn't get here fast enough. A few tables over, a baby in a stroller furiously waved his little arms and legs like a capsized beetle.

"So any advice?" Brenden's tone lowered.

A waiter dropped a heavy tray and the metal clatter rang out like an explosion.

The paper napkin was in shreds. Nick dropped it on the seat beside him, then he shrugged. "It might be too soon."

"Nah." Brenden shook his head, gulped down the rest of his drink, and then wiped his mouth with the back of his hand. "We've been dating for over a year. It's *way* past time."

"Then why not just ask her?"

"I would, but I don't want to scare her off..." He rubbed the back of his neck with stiff fingers. "I love her, dude."

"Good for you." Nick sighed again. "Now can we please just get through lunch without all the *touchy-feelies*?"

***

If you've compared the two examples, then you can grasp how I wove in all the key elements needed to make a scene more tangible by adding Deeper POV, which includes "character voice," setting, and sensory details.

Even dialogue heavy scenes need some type of connection to the setting, so the reader can visualize the world in-which your characters populate. When describing the surroundings, I would include some visual elements, like the weather, or some of the five senses, or colors to make the setting come alive for the reader.

Some of writers might've noticed that I added internal-thoughts to the second example too because when a writer is *showing* rather than *telling*, it helps to heighten the scene with additional context to make the dialogue more visual.

Writers can easily revise any dialogue scenes with "talking heads" in their current manuscript by inserting facial expressions, gestures, actions, and tones of voice within the conversation to make it more realistic.

Also, the way a character speaks is an important part of making the story more lifelike and *show* the character's personality, so try not to be too formal in the speech.

Also, I'm not stating that writers can't use dialogue tags. Just use them in moderation. Remember that dialogue and Deep POV and action accelerate the story, while introspection (internal-babbling) and exposition will slow it down. Action, tension, and dialogue are the best solutions to revising any pages of straight exposition that go on for longer than a page in your manuscript.

INTERNAL EXPOSITION

Quote: "Dialogue is a key part of any story and it's usually what readers find most engrossing. They might skim long descriptions, but when they get to someone speaking, that's where they'll get pulled back into the narrative."—*Moody Writing blog, mooderino*

Internal exposition is when a character is busy having a discussion inside their own head. It can provide vital information on how a character is reacting or feeling in regards to what's happening within the story, but it's a skill that if done incorrectly, often causes shallower writing or narrative distance.

Dialogue illustrates characterization quicker than any amount of exposition. If you disrupt the action and dialogue to include colossal chunks of detailed description or introspection, it will remove the reader from the story.

Yet, if I'm being honest, I have to admit that I've written a couple of bad novels, and even had them published under a pen name many years ago. But that was long before I sharpened my writing skills and studied the art of fiction writing with a crazed intensity. I read articles on editing and revision, books on the craft, and studied style guides. I love learning new ways to improve my writing, so a writer at any stage in their career should gleam some insight from this chapter.

Long blocks of introspection can be dreary and slow down the pacing of a novel because it is passive, and often robs the reader of getting to know a character's personality and/or personal struggles by *showing* them.

While dialogue usually quickens the pace of the story, internal exposition slows it down.

So anytime a writer can revise introspection into dialogue, they should. Especially, when there are two or more characters in a scene.

Why have the character say it in his/her head, when it would be much more impactful to be shown in conversation?

Please carefully study this example…

SHALLOW: Henry said that he wanted to quit school. I wondered what Henry meant by that remark. Was he serious about dropping out of college?

REVISED: "I'm thinking about quitting school next semester," Henry said, shuffling his feet.

"Why would you do that?" I leaned back to stare into his face. "Are you *serious* about dropping out of college?"

Henry stared out the window and didn't answer.

INTERNAL EXPOSITION

***

The revised example reveals more insight into the characters, rather than having the main character just thinking about it in his/her head.

Inner-monologue is one of the essential ingredients used to create a comprehensive storyline. Unfortunately, it's all too often one of the most misused elements in storytelling. Since internal-monologue is slower and can be boring for the reader, find ways to bring it to life through Deep POV, action, and dialogue by revising it into *showing* rather than *telling*. Don't let your character's mental babble (long blocks of introspection) go on for pages at a time without a break by either dialogue or action.

Whenever possible, I encourage writers to revise introspection (also known as internal exposition, interior monologue, inner-thoughts, or inner -ialogue, etc.) into dialogue when there are more than two characters in a scene. I feel that dialogue is naturally faster paced and much more interesting to readers than long blocks of narrative.

I have included some examples on how to stay in Deep POV by turning boring exposition into attention-grabbing dialogue between the characters.

(In the shallow examples, I have underlined what I consider shallower writing (telling).) Please carefully compare these sentences...

SHALLOW: I <u>saw</u> the pirate give me a <u>mean look</u> as he asked about his gold.

DEEP POV: The pirate's bushy brows furrowed. "Where be my gold, wench?"

SHALLOW: Martha McCray was <u>angry</u> and glared at me. I <u>told her</u> that I wasn't scared of her, but that was a lie.

DEEP POV: Martha McCray gave me the evil eye and I gave it right back to her. "You don't scare me," I lied.

SHALLOW: Damon wore a <u>furious expression</u>, and then he told Tyler that he was going to beat him up.

DEEP POV: Damon's expression darkened as he rolled up his sleeves. "I hope you realize, I'm about to kick your ass, Tyler."

SHALLOW: Klaus stared at Stefan and he <u>looked upset</u> when he called him a liar and accused him of dating Caroline.

DEEP POV: Klaus skewed him with a hard, unblinking stare. "You lied! You *are* dating, Caroline."

SHALLOW: Emily <u>felt angry</u>. Why did he have to be such a jerk?

DEEP POV: Emily's lips flatten and she gets right in his face. "Why do you have to be such a jerk?"

SHALLOW: He <u>looked unsympathetic</u> when he said that he would not help me bury the corpse.

INTERNAL EXPOSITION

DEEP POV: His expression turned stony. "I'm *not* helping you bury the body. You're on your own this time."

SHALLOW: He was <u>exasperated</u> with the cops and demanded that they locate his daughter.

DEEP POV: He ground his teeth. "Find my daughter—*now!*"

SHALLOW: Amber <u>looked indifferent</u> when she complained that I always got my way.

DEEP POV: "Fine. Have it *your* way. You always do," she said, her tone laced with bitterness.

SHALLOW: Dorian <u>appeared mad</u> at her for asking if they could eat pasta again this evening.

DEEP POV: Dorian clenched his mouth tighter. "I do *not* want to eat pasta again tonight."

***

Writers never want the reader to feel removed from their story by too much introspection, instead of being deeply emerged within the fictional world that the author has worked so hard to create. Now I realize that writers can't turn all introspection into dialogue, but I encourage you to find clever ways to change the ones that you can.

CRAFTING GREAT DIALOGUE

Quote: "*Real People Don't Have Long Monologues. I know you want to show off your exquisite writing skills with a long speech, but in normal situations, real people don't like making speeches. They feel uncomfortable when they're the only one talking for a long time. If you want to write a speech, you need to create some kind of excuse for your character to give the speech. Perhaps he just won an award or he's about to go on a long trip or he's dying and wants to share his last words or he's a priest and he gives speeches every Sunday...*" —*author Joe Bunting from 16 Observations About real Dialogue*

Writing realistic dialogue does not come easily to everyone. Well-written dialogue advances the story and reveals insight into characterization, while providing a respite from lengthy sections of introspection and it also helps to avoid author intrusion.

However, just as natural sounding dialogue is one of the most powerful tools at a writer's disposal, nothing jerks the reader out of a story quicker than badly written dialogue or a conversation drowning with too many various dialogue tags. Deviating too much beyond "said tags" only brings unwanted attention to the tags and you want the reader's to focus on your brilliantly written dialogue, not your ability to think of synonyms for "said" or "asked."

As I already mentioned, almost all of your dialogue scenes need some tension, conflict, and emotion. As you revise, remember that too many dialogue tags slaughter the flow of a natural conversation, and often reek of author intrusion. The overuse of dialogue tags can also create the dreaded narrative distance.

Another helpful tip to remember as writers revise their stories, is that if they're adding backstory to the dialogue, it should *never* be obvious to the reader that they're being fed important facts or information. Writers don't have to tell the reader everything up front with info-dumps of backstory in the dialogue, either.

Using descriptive tags instead of saidisms can also reveal a character's appearance—what a character wears, his/her physical characteristics, and even describe body language. Remember, real people don't just sit and have a conversation—they lean forward, cross their arms, scratch their heads, and fidget.

And try to remove most of the tags that end with a "ly" adverb. Instead, rewrite the dialogue with an action, facial expression, or some description as an alternative. If the dialogue is written well enough, you'll only need to use a few "said" tags within the conversation.

Unlike other tags, "said" is generally invisible to readers. And please don't use verbs to describe an emotion, and then try to turn it into a dialogue tag. Real people don't frown, smirk, chuckle, sneer, hiss, seethe, pout, or frown in a conversation.

Wrong example:

He laughed, "Stop tickling me."

"You'll all die tonight," Jake sneered.

Correct example:

He laughed. "Stop tickling me!"

"You'll all die tonight." Jake sneered.

***

Now when writing a scene, which has multiple characters, writers will need to make sure that they do include some type of tag to indicate which character is speaking. Without any forms of tags, a reader can become easily confused and frustrated. And having too many can weigh down your dialogue and kill your pacing.

I have provided an example from an early draft of my novel, IMMORTAL ECLIPSE to help you get a clear idea on how to write dialogue from multiple characters' perspective.

The first dialogue example is of a "weak" scene overloaded with dialogue tags, formal, stiff speech, and too many exclamation points. (In the shallow example, I have underlined what I consider shallower writing (telling) and obtrusive "ly" adverbs.)

In an early draft, it is okay to insert shallow writing and dialogue tags. Once you start revisions on the third or fourth draft, that is when it is time to go back and polish a scene with a Deeper POV, setting descriptions, and sensory details.

Please carefully study this scene…

SHALLOW:

I <u>watch</u> as a tall man <u>looks</u> at the group, but I can't hear what he says. I lean my ear closer to the door and then I <u>look</u> inside the room to <u>watch</u> them.

"It cannot merely be a coincidence," Mrs. Pratt <u>states confusedly</u>.

"Naturally, it is not!" Scarface <u>replies snarkily</u>.

"I could scarcely believe it when I saw her." I <u>see</u> William <u>look</u> at the tall man with the long scar. "Is that the reason she's here, Victor?"

Victor replies, "She is the *one* we've been waiting for!"

I <u>wonder</u> if they are talking about me or someone else.

I <u>watch as</u> Mrs. Pratt crosses her legs and then she <u>looks</u> at Joshua, who sits across from her on a sofa.

"Are you sure it will work this time?" William <u>asks warily</u>.

I <u>wonder</u> what William is talking about, but he's going to wear out the rug's fabric with his pacing, I <u>think to myself</u>.

"Don't be ridiculous! Just look at her," Victor says angrily. "I have checked the reference again. It *will* work!"

I notice that William stops pacing and I see him cross his arms. "Good. Because this is the last time I will partake in this madness!"

"Do *not* tell me you've suddenly developed a conscience." Victor looks around slowly, but I notice that nobody meets his gaze. They appear uneasy and look at the floor.

"Keep your voices down," Mrs. Pratt says sternly.

Victor looks angry now. He looks toward Mrs. Pratt. "Mother? Your thoughts?"

I never knew the housekeeper had a son, I thought.

"There's no doubt she is the one we have been hoping for all these years," Mrs. Pratt says softly.

Victor appears excited. "I knew it!"

I hear Joshua sigh. "And you are sure the girl can survive the ritual?"

"Well, of course!" Victor scoffs loudly.

*　*　*

The second dialogue example below is the final draft of the same scene, and it has been rewritten with less dialogue tags and with some action, Deep POV, and description laced throughout the narrative to convey which character is speaking. This example creates a more riveting scene for the reader.

Please thoroughly study this revised scene…

DEEP POV:

Scarface addresses the group, but I can't hear what he says. I lean my ear closer to the door.

"It can't merely be a coincidence," Mrs. Pratt says, leaning forward.

"Naturally, it isn't," Scarface replies with a smirk.

"I could scarcely believe it when I saw her." William faces the tall man with the long scar. "Is that the reason she's here, Victor?"

Victor aka Scarface nods. "She's the *one* we've been waiting for."

My sixth sense flares high, then quickly dies down. Are they talking about me?

Mrs. Pratt crosses her legs and glances at Joshua, who sits across from her on the matching chintz sofa. The sofas face each other from either side of the fireplace, an Oriental rug covering the hardwood floor between them.

"Are you sure it will work this time?" William asks.

I have no idea what William's talking about, but he's going to wear out the rug's fabric with his pacing.

"Don't be ridiculous! Just look at her," Victor says, twisting to face William. His jaw tenses. "I've even checked the reference again. It *will* work."

William stops pacing and crosses his arms. "Good. Because this is the last time I'll partake in this madness."

"Do *not* tell me you've suddenly developed a conscience." Victor gazes around slowly, like a cobra watching for careless mice, but nobody meets his gaze. They're all too busy staring at the floor.

Apparently, there's something more interesting within the patterns of the rug than Victor and his snark.

"Keep your voices down," Mrs. Pratt says sternly.

After leveling William with a long glare, Victor turns to Mrs. Pratt. "Mother? Your thoughts?"

No way. The grumpy housekeeper has a son?

"There's no doubt she's the one we've been hoping for all these years, dearest," Mrs. Pratt says.

Victor clasps his hands together. "I knew it!"

Joshua sighs. "And you're sure the girl can survive the ritual?"

Victor scoffs. "Well, of course!"

***

Writing scenes with multiple characters is hard, but you *must* try to remember to identify each speaker or the reader will get lost. It is okay to add dialogue tags like "said or say or says" because they are invisible to the reader, but it helps them to recognize who said what.

Now try to revise a scene from your own work that features a large cast of characters and you'll notice a wonderful difference!

INSERTING TENSION

Quote: "Dialogue is one of the hardest parts of fiction to write, because it needs to sound real while also performing its job within the story. One task given to dialogue is to reveal more about the personality of each character in the story, by showing how they talk and how they interact with other characters. Studying examples of fictional dialogue that works can help you develop an ear for how dialogue reveals more about the characters." —*author, Bonnie Way*

I suggest that writers revise every section of dialogue until the reader can actually envisage the characters and hear their voices through what they say and *how* they say it. Remember that ALL dialogue needs tension, conflict, and emotion.

To make dialogue sound more authentic, try to remove what some editors refer to as: *Slider Words* from your dialogue. These are all the: "Oh" or "Well" or "Okay" "You know" and "But" words that often begin a line of dialogue. These overused words help a writer *slide* into the dialogue, but you can usually cut those overworked words from your writing. At times, there is a

INSERTING TENSION

need for a beat or a pause, but a slider word is almost certainly *not* the way to do write it.

Don't let your dialogue become too predictable or unoriginal!

This longer example was taken from my published novel, SHATTERED SILENCE should help give you some ideas on how to create tension, mood, and conflict in your dialogue scenes.

Please study this scene…

As he walked into the kitchen to get a drink, I caught Darrah staring at Trent with intense eyes. When Aunt Lauren slid up beside Darrah, I casually moved behind them, and pretended to fiddle with the paper plates, staying within earshot.

"Sooo, I wonder why Maxwell Donovan finally returned after all these years," Aunt Lauren said.

"What are you implying?" Darrah's tone was low, malicious.

"*Please*. You know exactly what I'm implying." Aunt Lauren's face contorted into a scowl.

"Who invited you anyway?"

Aunt Lauren smiled sweetly. "Why, your handsome husband, dear sister."

"I'll bet," Darrah said through clenched teeth. "So you thought you'd show up after all these years and try to rattle me? *Pathetic*." Her eyes flashed with outrage. "And stay away from my husband."

Aunt Lauren flinched. "Why?" she demanded, her tone frosty and exact. "Should I tell him that you used spells and trickery to win him over, little sister?"

"How dare you speak to me like that," Darrah said, her tone sharp enough to cut a diamond. She seemed incensed that her sister would dare chastise her.

"Watch yourself. Before I tell *her* the truth." Aunt Lauren's eyes narrowed. "We all know—you try to steal what isn't yours." She shrugged, and her tone became deadly quiet. "One day, the truth will be exposed. And I can't wait to watch you squirm."

Darrah prowled around Aunt Lauren, her aura darkened with a deepness older than night. In her dainty hand, a glass of wine was in danger of spilling. "Truth? I'm the only one who has made sacrifices. I'm the one stuck doing the family duty because you were found incompetent."

"Duty? To the coven—maybe, but *not* to your own flesh and blood. Your own daughter."

"I have no idea what you're talking about." Darrah picked invisible lint off her dress. Her cheeks each grew a splotch of bright red, like a drop of blood on a single white rose. She glared hard at her older sister, her face contorting into something unnatural and ugly, and her voice became a hiss. "The years haven't been kind to you, Lauren. Your magic has become feeble."

Aunt Lauren snorted. "Hardly," she said in a menacing voice. Then she stepped back and eyed Darrah with disgust. "God, we

INSERTING TENSION

are such opposites. You worked black magick and risked your soul pursuing a man. And I was forced to give up the one man that I loved, and now I am surrounded by white magic. Ironic, if you ask me."

***

Remember that each character should have their own distinctive dialogue, which means "character voice." Another one way to do this is by creating mannerisms. Most people have at least a few verbal habits that are unique to them.

For example, an old friend of mine developed the habit of inserting the word "basically" into nearly every sentence that came out of her mouth. One of my characters in my YA series, always uses the word "dude" in his dialogue. Just make sure to remember which characters have certain habits or verbal cues.

INTENSIFYING CONFLICT

Quote: "*Dialogue is an Expression of Character.* Dialogue is the impression of how people speak in real life, but actually much more interesting, with more forward motion. Dialogue is one of the core elements of storytelling, and it needs to be used well. Dialogue is an expression of character, background, education, locality, and circumstance. Listen to how people talk and you'll see that who they are and the situation they find themselves in will influence what they say and how they say it..." ~*author and blogger, Katherine Cowley*

Dialogue is all about expressing character traits through either internal or external conflict.

All dialogue should achieve at least one of the subsequent three things:

Progress the storyline.

Offer new information for the reader.

Provide insight into characterization.

Push the plot forward.

INTENSIFYING CONFLICT

Give the reader a break from exposition.

Let's start with conflict/tension. If there is no tension within some of the dialogue scenes, then the conversation might need to be revised. The tension can often be internal (he's concealing a secret from her or she doesn't trust him) or external (a windstorm is whirling gust at the two of them or someone has hacked her computer). Yet, it has to be there.

Dialogue can illustrate a character's temperament quicker than any amount of exposition. However, only if you give your characters something interesting to talk about, something that pushes your story forward, which means revising with conflict or tension.

And remember as you revise that we all react differently to situations. So will your characters, both inwardly, externally, and in their dialogue.

This next excerpt was taken from my published novel, BEAUTIFULLY BROKEN, and shows how writers can include tension, emotion, action, and even conflict into a dialogue scenes.

Please carefully study this example...

Trudging towards the double-doors, I lifted the strap of my backpack over one shoulder. Outside the cool air glided across my skin and I attempted to clear my mind. But it was no good.

At the Jeep, I pulled the keys from my pocket. Just as I was about to insert the key into the lock, a disturbance shifted the air. Spinning around, I held my key out like a weapon, poised to attack.

"What are you going to do? Stab me with your key?"

Speechless, my gaze swept over Trent, taking in his low-slung jeans and snug cotton T-shirt.

A smirk touched his lips. "Did I frighten you?"

Yes!

"No. What're you doing here?"

"I was on my way home when I saw your Jeep parked in the lot."

Yeah, right. Probably looking for Brittany. Your stupid girlfriend.

Frowning, I narrowed my eyes. "How did you even know it's my Jeep?"

"I have my sources," he said with a sly smile.

Stalker much?

The backpack slid from my shoulder to the ground. "Oh, yeah?" I crossed my arms. "And what do these so-called sources tell you about me?"

"Lots of interesting tidbits…"

"Like?" I asked.

Trent didn't answer, instead he took a step forward, leaning in close to my ear like a lover about to whisper sweet-nothings, and I pressed my back tightly against the Jeep. I was pinned and at his mercy.

Slowly, he lifted his hand and gently tucked loose hair behind my ear. His breath grazed over the sensitive skin on my neck and I trembled. Trent stood so close that his cologne, an intoxicating scent of sandalwood that mingled with his natural scent, invaded my senses. I could hardly move, barely breathe as his fingertips trailed from my ear to caress the curve of my neck. Unable to look away, I felt trapped in his gaze. Lost in the gold flecks of his intense emerald stare, a look that revealed raw desire and, for a slight moment, a flicker of what looked like hope.

Swallowing hard, I tried to ignore the lusty sensations curling my toes and sparking like electricity throughout my body. I had the strong urge to kiss him, to slip my hands under his shirt and run my palms over his muscular chest.

Instead, I shoved him away. "Stop it, Trent."

He smiled, white teeth glinting in the speckled sunlight. "Stop what? What am I doing?"

"You know *exactly* what you're doing," I said. "Making me feel all confused and tingly..." I clamped my mouth shut.

Trent smiled wider, his eyes crinkling at the corners. "Is that what I'm doing? Then why should I stop, *mon coeur*?"

What was with him? Talk about mood swings. He acted stand-offish after we kissed and now he was trying to make the moves on me in the school parking lot.

"Because I'm not that easy to win over. And I'm *really* not in the mood to play whatever game it is you're playing." I opened the Jeep's door and threw my backpack onto the passenger seat. "Try your lines on Brittany. She might be interested, but I'm not."

***

By reading that excerpt, did it spark your own creative muse? Do you see now how much fun writing dialogue can be?

Find clever ways to spice up your dialogue!

Modern readers in general prefer a story that moves at a steady pace. If not, they soon get bored. Too much dialogue without any breaks can make the reader become lost and disoriented.

And too much non-stop chattering from your characters can be frustrating, so break up the long by tossing in some gestures or description to spice things up. Have the other character ask a question or interrupt.

Often writers need to use *tough love* while revising to trim down any longer sections of dialogue that add nothing to the storyline so that the plot can progress at a faster pace.

REALISTIC CONVERSATIONS

Quote: "*Read the dialogue aloud.* This is the #1 tip that will solve 90% of your problems if you pay attention to how the words sound. Fix the awkward syntax, the too perfect grammar, the long-winded response. A breath unit is the number of syllables a reader would have to read aloud in one breath. Readers take breaths at punctuation marks. Try keeping to 20 syllables or fewer per breath unit (25 is pushing it), and vary the lengths. Too many long sentences make your reader lose his or her place. Too many short ones are choppy and jarring, like using exclamation points after each sentence." —*writer, editor and blogger, Lara Willard*

The most constructive tip that I offer fiction writers is to read the dialogue out loud. If writers pay close attention to how it sounds, then they will be able to easily spot most of the unnatural sounding speech in their dialogue scenes. If the character's conversation sounds stilted, boring, irrelevant, or otherwise ineffective when listening to it out loud, then it'll sound the same way to a reader when they read the novel.

Trust me on this, there is nothing that will bring out the flaws in a fiction manuscript easier than reading it out loud. Writers can listen to the narrative read by someone else, or even from the built-in voices on their own computer. While listening to a story read aloud, suddenly, all of those overused verbs, repeated words, stilted dialogue, typos, and awkward phrases will jump out at writers like snarling dogs.

There is some great and easy to use a free down-loadable text-to-speech software called Ultra HAL that can help. Then you just turn up your speakers, sit back, and listen to your novel. Hit pause when you encounter a mistake, open your document, edit, and then go back to listening.

Reading your manuscript aloud is one of the best ways to locate and fix any typos or misspelled words, too. (Even nonfiction writers should listen to the text read out loud to fix any errors.) Occasionally, I still print out a hard copy of my current manuscript for proofreading and editing, but I've found listening to the entire novel read verbally is an excellent alternative.

And listening to the manuscript being read aloud forces a writer to hear the rhythm, flow, and speech patterns, which is a *huge* help during proofreading and editing second or third drafts. Often times, dialogue reads fine on the document, but when a writer reads it out loud or listens to it, they will most often find that it doesn't sound realistic or natural.

Some writers even check through and edit their manuscript backward, page-by-page, which can be useful in spotting typos, grammar blunders, and even spelling mistakes.

My last piece of advice, wait until after you've finished edits on at least five drafts, had at least two experienced critique partners edit your manuscript, and you have read the entire text out loud, before contacting literary agents. Or even self-publishing your work.

Please look into hiring a professional freelance editor to critique your manuscript before publication. Don't submit your work before it's polished and tightened! Not that any of us *cough* have ever done that before.

Writers want to know an insider secret to writing better dialogue?

Turn your manuscript into a PDF doc (cute PDF is free) and have Adobe Reader (or any reader software) read your story for you. The voice may sound robotic, but again let me stress that listening to a story read aloud will help writers catch inaccuracies, help make dialogue scenes come alive, which are all things even the spellchecker can miss.

I personally use Natural Reader software, which is also free and you can download it onto to your computer. I stop the program whenever I catch something, and open up my word doc and fix it. Then go back to listening.

Another cool trick is when you read your dialogue out loud, listen to your voice as you say each line from your character's viewpoint.

Consider these questions:

What is your character's mood?

How does your character sound?

How do they speak?

My last bit of advice is to *always* listen to your manuscript read out loud. Writers will discover that they are their own best critic when a writer hears the words.

For all the aspiring writers who purchased this book, this manual should give you the inspiration to write great dialogue.

DIALOGUE DESCRIPTIONS

Quote: "*Use dialogue tags and actions effectively.* Dialogue loses all sense and purpose if readers can't follow who's saying what, so you'll need to make sure you effectively attribute (or 'tag') lines of dialogue to their speakers. The simplest and most common method, and the one generally championed by most literary types, is to use the word 'said'. It's clear, it's unobtrusive, and it doesn't feel forced or overly descriptive. When it comes down to it, it's a matter of personal preference, so if you prefer to mix things up a bit then feel free. But do keep in mind that, when in doubt, it's best to keep things simple…" —*Claire Bradshaw, freelance writer and editor*

This chapter focuses on the overuse of physical gestures and facial expressions that get used so much in dialogue scenes that they've become stale and boring. Always try to avoid clichéd action tags, overused emotional descriptors, and reusing the same facial expressions repeatedly to describe an emotion to keep the writing fresh and original. Writers may not even be conscious of writing them, but they should try to be aware of them now.

Don't get me wrong, by inserting a descriptive tag to illustrate a character's feelings and reactions through gestures or facial expressions instead of a dialogue "said" tag can help a scene come alive for the reader. Facial expressions and body language are vital components in order for the reader to have a clear visualize of what's going on in some of your scenes.

One simple technique that works is to actually consider how *you* would personally react to the situation. Would you laugh? Cry? Be angry? Shout? Feel a sense of loss?

Writers can *show* the reader more realistically what's going on in a scene, or a characters emotional reaction, or even what's *not* being said by using the Deep POV method within their dialogue heavy scenes.

Also, have you ever noticed that some people have repetitive gestures or nervous habits? For instance, when my friend Anna is speaking, she pushes her hair behind her ears. My mother, Karen, is very expressive and uses her hands a lot when she's talking. My friend Alex always leans forward when he's trying to make a point. He gets right into your personal space.

Some of your characters should have their own unusual nervous tics or unique gestures that only they use throughout your manuscript. But don't go crazy! Use Sparingly.

Even I am guilty of abusing this collection of overused generic tags listed below (or called dialogue beats).

Recently I went through my manuscript and removed all of them except one. I searched online for "reading body language,"

DIALOGUE DESCRIPTIONS

and "facial interpretations," and also, "gestures and their meanings" and "conveying emotion through dialogue." (These are all types of Deep POV.) Then I searched for differences in female and male behaviors and reactions in conversation. Research can be fun and enlightening. I discovered a lot of useful information.

If you must have a tag in a dialogue scene to make it more powerful and clear for the reader, then I want you to try to revise by using a different phrase instead of "shrugged" or "nodded" or "shook his/her head."

I bet you'll find some of these overused tags in almost every published novel:

Nodded or bobbed head

Smiled

Laughed

Shook head

Made a face

Shrugged

Frowned

Grimaced

Winced

Uttered or muttered or whispered

Cried or bellowed or shouted

Pouted

Scowled

Pursed or puckered lip

Stroked his chin or beard or cheek

Steeple fingers or clasp hands

Folded or crossed arms

Cleared throat

Swallowed

Raised eyebrows

Blush or flushed

Cleansing breath or breathe deeply or took deep breath

Hiss or hissed

There are so many other ways to describe nervousness other than clearing the throat or swallowing. Or showing surprise by raising eyebrows or wide eyes. Be imaginative and rewrite them into a completely different action or facial expression that still *shows* the character emotion or reaction through Deep POV.

Now I urge you to use the "Find" feature in your word processing program (Ctrl + F in Microsoft Word) to rewrite most of these overused descriptions. Be creative!

Well, that concludes my advice on writing great dialogue.

Wishing each and every one you much success on your writing journey!

BONUS READING

Read on for more inspiring tools and tips on writing and self-editing a page-turning novel from the other bestselling guidebooks in the *Fiction Writing Tools* series!

CHARACTER EMOTION

THE WRITER'S GUIDE TO CHARACTER EMOTION

Most writers struggle with creating a captivating story. The fastest way to improve your writing is by the use of the "Deep Point-of-View" technique, which can transform any novel from mediocre storytelling into riveting prose.

This manual will provide writers with the essential skills needed to significantly enhance their characterization and intensify emotions by eliminating filtering words that cause narrative distance. Plus, this unique guidebook includes hundreds of amazing ways to use "show don't tell" to submerge readers so deeply into any scene that they will experience the story along with the characters.

Writers will learn to:

*Revise Shallow Writing

*Deepen Characterization

*Craft Realistic Visceral Reactions

*Resolve Showing vs. Telling Issues

*Create Lifelike Character Expressions

Bestselling author, S. A. Soule also shares her expertise with writers on how to apply "showing" methods through powerful examples in action, along with the necessary tools to immediately deepen the reader's experience with vivid, sensory details.

Are you ready to instantly take your writing skills to the next level?

***

SHALLOW WRITING

Quote: "Rather than report on emotions (i.e., he was angry, he was scared) *show* them. Yes, it's the old show don't tell. But it's true. Deep POV is the ultimate in showing. Use action, thought, and perception to show emotion and feelings. When you're annoyed, it colors your whole perception of the world. Everyone on the damn road is too damn slow and every traffic light is out to get you. Show that." —*author and editor, Ann Laurel Kopchik*

Deep POV is getting your reader so deeply submerged within the head of your characters that they experience—*really experience*—what the character is feeling. One way to stay in close-and-personal (*show*, don't *tell*) is to do this: try to reduce as many filtering references as you can from your writing.

Instead, simply *show* us what the main character *felt* and *saw* and *heard* and *decided*, without using any filter words.

If a writer overuses filtering words that clutter up each sentence and remove the reader from the experience the character is undergoing or feeling, it creates narrative distance. Anything that describes the narrator's thought or mode of perception is considered "telling" the reader. If you can revise those sentences as much as possible, the POV will feel deeper and your prose will be greatly enhanced.

Also, if a critique partner or beta reader comments on something that confused them over the emotional reaction of one of your characters, check to make sure the stimulus cause is obvious to the reader through Deep POV. I advise to always try to include some type of an emotional response and a physical reaction to intensify the moment of any scene. This helps to *show* the character's response to what is happening by using the Deep POV method.

***

To really help you understand what Deep POV is and why it will turn your novel into an unputdownable read, I have compiled examples from my own published novels.

This excerpt was taken from my book, SHATTERED SILENCE, to offer an example of how to use this wonderful technique.

CHARACTER EMOTION

The first example is what I call shallow writing and crammed with filter words. (The filter words are underlined.)

Please compare the two illustrations below...

SHALLOW:

I could _feel_ my head throbbing, which _made_ me reluctant to open my eyes. I _could tell_ that my vision was blurry. I took deep breaths because I _felt_ dizzy and I _knew_ I wasn't strong enough to raise my head. I leaned on one elbow. My tongue _felt_ like it was glued to the roof of my mouth.

A door opened, and I _saw_ a tall woman, with short red hair, wearing dark blue scrubs and clogs. She was tough looking like a man, I _thought_.

"You're awake. I'm Nurse Gwen. Let me fetch the doctor." She turned around and closed the door, then locked it.

Collapsing on the thin mattress, I _looked around_ at my foreign surroundings. I _noticed_ stark white walls, a metal-framed bed, and a nightstand. _There was_ a solitary window with security wiring. I _heard_ a loudspeaker call out codes and someone yelled. I _saw_ a fluorescent light near the ceiling. I _could smell_ bleach from the bedding and the antiseptic scent _made_ me _feel_ nausea.

I have no memory of how I'd gotten here, I _thought_.

There were no shadows on the walls. But eventually I _knew_ they'd come for me. I _felt like_ I had no protection here. I _felt_ weak and _scared_.

I pulled off the sheets, and swung my legs over the bed. I was dressed in a hospital gown that <u>felt</u> scratchy and I had a bandage wrapped around my right wrist. I <u>noticed</u> that I had scrapes and bruises on my arms and legs. I could <u>see</u> a puncture wound on my arm where someone inserted a needle.

I <u>decided</u> to raise one hand to touch the gauze at my temple and <u>noticed</u> a white band on my left wrist: *Valley Grove Psychiatric Hospital: Trudell, Shiloh*

I <u>knew</u> then that I was in the hospital.

Now this second version is written in Deep POV, but it does contain one or two filter words for better flow. *Here's a revised version that reveals (shows), instead of tells...*

DEEP POV:

My head throbbed and I was reluctant to open my eyes. My vision blurry. I took deep breaths until the waves of dizziness lessened and I was strong enough to raise my head. I leaned on one elbow. My tongue felt glued to the roof of my mouth.

A door opened, admitting a tall lady—at least six feet—with short fiery-red hair, wearing dark blue scrubs and clogs. She looked tough and very butch. Bet nobody messed with her.

"You're awake. I'm Nurse Gwen. Let me fetch the doctor." She whipped around and closed the door. Locked it.

Collapsing on the thin mattress, I surveyed my foreign surroundings. Stark white walls, a metal-framed bed, and a nightstand. Solitary window with security wiring. Somewhere a

CHARACTER EMOTION

loudspeaker called out codes and someone howled loudly. Fluorescent light glared down from the ceiling. Whiffs of bleach wafted from the bedding and the antiseptic scent gave me nausea.

I had no memory of how I'd gotten here.

No shadows danced on the walls. But eventually they'd come for me. I had no protection here. I was weak. Defenseless. Vulnerable.

I yanked off the crisp sheets, and swung my legs over the cold metal bed. Someone had dressed me in a scratchy hospital gown and wrapped my right wrist in an elastic Ace bandage. I had scrapes and bruises on my arms and legs. My forearm had a puncture wound where someone had inserted a needle. I raised one hand to touch the gauze at my temple and gasped at the band on my left wrist that read: *Valley Grove Psychiatric Hospital: Trudell, Shiloh*

Oh, no! I was in the nut house!

***

When *telling*, the writer is making a statement. Readers are being told (telling) what to believe by the writer, rather than the readers discovering things for themselves.

Remember that these are just "guidelines" to help improve your skills as a writer. Occasionally breaking the 'rules' is what a story calls for. But don't do it too often. By trying to create meaningful, descriptive prose, it will naturally move the story forward and convey a richer experience for your reader. Don't weigh it down with filter words.

I'm assuming that since you purchased this handbook, it's because you want to improve your writing skills. If you use the Deep POV technique, I promise that you'll notice an amazing difference in your writing. And I bet your readers will, too!

DEEP POINT-of-VIEW METHOD

THE WRITER'S GUIDE TO CHARACTER EXPRESSION

The Fastest Way to Improve Dialogue, Settings, and Characterization!

No matter what genre you write, this second manual on the Deep Point of View technique should be kept as a vital reference in every writer's toolbox. This in-depth guide offers specific, practical tools for creative fiction writers on how to craft realistic settings, visceral responses, and lifelike characters.

Crammed with even more examples and ways to eliminate shallow writing, this book provides the necessary techniques to master describing facial expressions, body language, and character emotions. This resource of endless inspiration will reveal how to *dig deeper* to "show don't tell," which is essential to crafting compelling dialogue, vivid scenes, and deepening characterization.

Learn to write:

*Realistic settings through sensory details

*Three-dimensional characters

*Memorable "character voice"

*Authentic facial expressions

*Engaging dialogue

Bestselling author, S. A. Soule shares her expertise with writers by providing surefire, simple methods of getting readers so emotionally invested in their stories that booklovers will be flipping the pages to find out what happens next.

Are you ready to start improving your writing skills today?

***

CHARACTERIZATION

Quote: "...Voice is the "secret power" of great writing." —*Bestselling author, James Scott Bell*

Using the methods outlined in this chapter will help writers create three-dimensional characters who will come alive within their complex fictional worlds by captivating their readers with deeper layers of characterization.

One of the critical elements to differentiate good writing from just average storytelling relates to how the writer handles the point-of-view. That's why, I strongly feel that Deep POV is tightly connected to *voice,* which is a big part of characterization in my opinion.

In this chapter, I'll try my best to explain "voice" in the terms that I understand them, and clarify how important it is to convey that through Deeper POV.

I consider the phrase "show, don't tell" to primarily specify going deeper into a character's POV. It isn't just stating the facts or information, but giving the reader a glimpse of the world through the senses of the POV character. It allows the reader to become more immersed within the storyline and feel a stronger connection to the character(s).

A lot of manuscripts that I've edited over the years were lacking any "voice." So it is my belief that some writers don't fully comprehend what it means, or how it can deepen the characterization and give your writing a distinctive style.

So let me put it this way…just as everyone has their own characteristic way of speaking or expressing themselves, a writer's characters should also have a distinctive "voice" that clearly comes across in the narrative.

I advise the writers that I work with to strengthen "voice" by using phrasing that reflects the overall tone of their book, along with the POV character's unique personality. How the character reacts or responds in any given situation should be distinctive to their individuality. So choose your nouns and verbs carefully. Being specific about even small details like the weather, description of settings, or objects can create a stronger impression of that character's POV.

These next two longer scenes were each taken from one of my novels, UNDER SUNLESS SKIES. The first one lacks any real emotional descriptions and has no "voice." (I have underlined what I consider to be shallower writing.)

Please carefully compare these examples…

SHALLOW:

I really hate my boring math class. I'm not listening to Mrs. Brooks talk about angles and measurements because I do not care. I will never use this type of math in the real world. I <u>look up at the clock</u>. There is fifteen minutes before the bell rings.

I <u>feel bored and sleepy</u>. I put my elbows on my desktop, and then I put my forehead into my hands and I close my eyes. Mrs. Brooks continues to talk about equations and her loud voice is <u>irritating</u>.

"If Miss Masterson paid attention in class," Mrs. Brooks says, "I wouldn't have to re-explain how the trigonometric ratios are derived from triangle similarity considerations today."

I don't glance up, because I don't want to <u>see her ugly face</u>.

"Are you paying attention, Miss Masterson, or are you in a world of your own again?"

I <u>hear</u> several students laugh. I <u>feel</u> my cheeks <u>heat with embarrassment</u>.

I still do not <u>look</u> up at her unattractive features. "No, I'm not preoccupied," I say <u>sullenly</u>.

DEEP POINT-of-VIEW METHOD

"Then would you like to share with the class what you were doing that is more important than listening to my lecture?" Mrs. Brooks asks <u>impatiently</u>.

Now I <u>feel enraged</u> as I lift my head. My classmates laugh, and I <u>hear</u> them move in their seats as they turn to look at me.

***

The revised scene has been revised with Deep POV and it has "voice," tension-soaked dialogue, introspection, and characterization. It is much longer and more detailed, but creates a much more vivid scene in the reader's mind.

Please study this rewritten example...

DEEP POV:

Now I'm trapped sitting in class, not really listening to Mrs. Longwinded Brooks drone on about angles and measurements. I glare at the back of Hayden's head, silently willing him to turn around and acknowledge me. It feels like I'm a minor character being faded out of a TV series, as if I've had one minute of total screen time with Hayden.

Clenching my jaw, every muscle in my body feels taut. I *hate* how he just blew me off. I *hate* that my parents aren't trustworthy. I *hate* Zach and his fat-shaming slurs. I *hate* the mysterious person leaving threats in my locker. And I *hate* this uncomfortable metal desk with gum stuck to the side of it.

The seconds tick by. I glance at the clock hanging on the wall. Thirty-nine tortuous minutes before class ends. I want to be anywhere but here. I almost wish demons would attack the school and drag me to Hell, or worse…somewhere where there's no chocolate. Now that would be pure evil!

Mrs. Brooks lectures on equations and her shrill voice sounds like braying sheep in heat. A sharp throbbing spreads across my forehead. I rest my elbows on the desk, then lower my head into my palms and close my eyes.

"If Miss Masterson would be more attentive…" Mrs. Brooks walks down the aisle, the rubber soles of her cheap pumps squeaking on the floor. "Then I wouldn't have to waste everyone's time by re-explaining how the trigonometric ratios derive from triangle similarity considerations." Her footsteps pause at my desk.

I keep my head down, my eyes squeezed shut. If I lift my head and look at her, I'll be compelled to stare at that mole on her chin. The one with the long, black witch hair sticking out of it.

"Are you paying attention, Miss Masterson?" She taps an impatient foot, then moves further along the aisle. "I do *not* tolerate sleeping in my classroom."

Jeez. Adults think they're *so* superior all the time. Just like my lying-deceiving parents.

"You do know that it's not Halloween, right?" Emma says in a loud whisper, twisting in her seat. "You look like a wannabe vampire in that strange getup."

The sarcastic edge in her voice grates on my last nerve.

With my head still cradled in my hands, I'm feeling the height of bitchiness coming on strong. So my style's dark with a side of edgy? What's the issue?

Slowly, I lift my head and shoot Emma a heated glare. "If you must know, it's Halloween *every* day at my house."

Emma's pink mouth gapes, then snaps shut. Most of my classmates turn in their seats to watch the impending showdown. Several kids even stop scribbling in their notebooks. Hayden hangs his head and shakes it as if in disapproval.

"You call *that* style? More like chubby couture." Emma snickers. "You must've read one too many Anne Rice novels. Unless you're praying you'll never come in contact with direct sunlight."

My cheeks heat, my skin piping so hot it feels as if I've stuck my face in an oven.

Several students giggle. Hayden's shoulders stiffen. Emma smiles and her best friend Kaitlyn rolls her squinty eyes.

I wonder if Emma is the blackmailer. Or maybe it's her evil sidekick, Kaitlyn. Their combined Sloane-hate places them on my *Do Not Trust* list. I size Emma up. She's wearing what might be the most preppy outfit I've ever seen outside an 80's Brat Pack movie, a white button-up shirt under a pink cardigan and capris with plaid flats. She almost looks too innocent to be a suspect, but her bitchiness is singeing through her good girl persona.

"Emma, cut it out," Hayden says under his breath.

Mrs. Brooks crosses both arms over her chest, obviously expecting me to apologize. "Are you quite done disrupting my class, Miss Masterson?"

Usually, I'm incapable of making people feel bad. Even if they're in the process of mocking me. Not today.

"Yeah, can I go back to taking my nap now?" I yawn, then mumble, "As if I'll ever use this stupid math anyway."

"Get out of my classroom!" Mrs. Brooks points an index finger at the door. "Go to the principal's office."

***

Besides all the other key ingredients a writer needs to enhance a scene, "voice" is among the most vital to Deeper POV. Spend some time getting to know your characters. Fill out character interviews and profiles to gain some insight into their temperaments and personalities, and then let that shine through in your narrative by use of the Deep POV technique.

Each character's voice personifies more than their speech or internal-thoughts. The narrative should express it as well. When you write a scene in a certain character's POV, each sentence in that scene has to read as though it is being experienced, felt, and expressed by that character.

One easy way to add "voice" to any character is to incorporate a few personal quirks, or unique phrases, rather than impersonal or formal syntax. Strive to include words meaningful to the character's personality and world views within the storyline.

VIVID SETTINGS AND CHARACTERS

THE WRITER'S GUIDE TO VIVID SETTINGS AND CHARACTERS

Learn to Describe a Realistic Setting with Atmospheric Detail and Create Vivid Characters!

No matter what genre you write, fiction writers will learn how to craft descriptions like a seasoned pro. World-building isn't easy, but creating original depictions of characters, locations, weather, and mood can greatly enhance anyone's writing.

Evocative settings are more effective and compelling when they're visible, auditory, olfactory, and tactile. And character descriptions are much more visual and lifelike when they have unique physical attributes.

This valuable reference and descriptive thesaurus offers writers a simplified way to depict vibrant settings and dynamic character descriptions flawlessly.

Writers will learn:

* The importance of using sensory details

* To expertly master showing vs. telling

* The impact setting can have on a story

* To effectively describe vivid characters

* How adding color will strengthen description

Each chapter provides specific, practical tools to help make writing descriptions and crafting three-dimensional characters simple and fun, with plenty of illustrations to highlight each point.

Bestselling author, S. A. Soule shares her expertise with writers by revealing foolproof, easy methods of getting readers so emotionally invested in the story that booklovers will be flipping the pages to find out what happens next. This in-depth guidebook should be kept as a vital reference in every writer's toolbox.

Are you ready to take your writing skills to the next level?

***

WRITING DESCRIPTION

Quote: "Try to cut down on your adjectives and adverbs. Modifiers don't specify words as much as you might think. More often than not, they actually abstract a thought, so sentences that rely on modifiers for descriptive strength are building on faulty foundations. You'll be more successful if you instead find the

VIVID SETTINGS AND CHARACTERS

verb that perfectly portrays the image you're envisioning. When you edit your work, spend considerable time scrutinizing your sentences to make sure the action maximizes full descriptive potential." —*editor and writer, Jon Gingerich*

If you've finished writing a novel or short story, then congratulations! That is a huge accomplishment to be very proud of, but now comes the revision work that will *really* make your story shine…

This book should help writers create dramatic scenes and illustrate how to craft a distinct and realistic world filled with three-dimensional characters, vivid locations, and naturalistic weather. Throughout this guide, writers will learn how they can use the five senses to arouse the reader's own senses of sight, touch, hear, smell, taste, and even feel. I'll even illustrate ways a writer of any genre can revise boring description info-dumps into a mood that harmonizes nicely with the novel's storyline, and how to craft unique descriptions of characters, locations, and climate.

Each chapter provides specific, practical tools to help make writing descriptions and crafting lifelike characters simple and fun, with plenty of examples to highlight each point.

The writing tools provided in this book cover many topics, such as:

* The importance of using sensory details

* How nouns and verbs impact description

* A thesaurus of descriptive words

* How to revise description info-dumps of places and characters

* How to expertly master showing vs. telling

* The impact setting can have on a story

* How to effectively describe life-like characters

* How adding color will strengthen descriptions

* How using the weather can create mood and atmosphere

* How the five senses can enhance the narrative

* How nature can enrich the background

Any fiction writer who has taken a creative writing course, received a professional edit on their manuscript, or worked with a critique partner has undoubtedly heard these three words: *show, don't tell.*

In my opinion, fiction is mostly about establishing a visceral, emotional connection between the character(s) and the reader. One way to do this is by *showing* instead of *telling.* Writers can use the Deep POV method to *show*, which creates vibrant and dramatic images within the reader's mind that will deeply immerse them in any fictional world.

Personally, I love writing descriptions of settings and characters, but as a freelance fiction editor, the majority of writers that I've worked with forget to include any details regarding the setting or their characters. While I'm reading and critiquing their work, I'm not connecting to the story if I can't envision the setting (where the story unfolds or where a scene happens) or even the characters themselves.

Description isn't optional in fiction. Every scene should include some details pertaining to the environment. It's imperative to effective world-building. If writers can make the settings original and colorful, the description will infuse your fictional world with mood and atmosphere.

For instance, if a new scene starts with two characters talking, but there's no mention of where the scene takes place or where the characters are, then it leaves me with a weak visual. Writers don't need to go into too much detail, but some is helpful in order to cement the scene and keep the characters from seeming as though they're floating around in space instead of being firmly anchored to the fictional world where they exist.

In the early drafts of a manuscript, *telling* is expected. It's more important to get the story finished and the plot holes filled in, then to worry about if a writer is *showing* enough. It's during the revision stage of later drafts (more like draft five or six) when it's time to polish the settings, include character descriptions, and check for red flags of *telling* throughout the narrative.

Writers should want readers to experience the story through the senses of their characters. And by engaging the five senses, it helps readers connect more closely with the character's experience. Shallow sentences with filter words will have the opposite effect.

Please compare these descriptive examples…

SHALLOW: I <u>touched</u> the dress to <u>feel</u> the fabric.

SHOWING: My fingers caressed the silky fabric.

If you're going to describe how something tastes, sounds and looks, then you can leave out how it feels and smells. You never want to assault your reader's senses, or they will skip ahead to get back to the action.

Please compare the next two examples…

SHALLOW: When Scott <u>heard</u> the growling <u>sound</u>, he <u>looked</u> down and <u>saw</u> a large dog blocking the trail. He <u>knew</u> it would attack if he moved. Scott <u>felt</u> a sense of <u>terror</u> build in his heart.

SHOWING: Scott halted at the warning growl. Standing in front of him was a large dog, flashing its teeth. He stifled the girlish shriek that leaked from his lips with one hand. Scott took a stumbling step backward, his heart jackhammering in his chest.

***

In the second example, you can imagine much more easily the dog and Scott's emotional response. It's always better to attempt to make your scene unique by inserting some of the five senses into the narrative.

To encourage fiction writers to craft stunning scenes, vivid characters, and lush settings, I have included references from my own personal database of descriptions in this guidebook. And I have created lots of examples to demonstrate how writers can avoid narrative distance in easy to grasp methods that can instantly improve anyone's writing.

Throughout this guide, I'll be discussing how writers can enhance elements of a story in any genre by incorporating a description of the locations, landscapes, and characters in each scene, with several simple techniques for creating sensory details to enhance the world-building.

PLOTTING A NOVEL

THE WRITER'S GUIDE TO PLOTTING A NOVEL

Awesome Tips on Crafting a Riveting Story that instantly Grabs Your Reader...

This manual offers amazing techniques for creating stronger beginnings and ways to write a page-turning plot for your fiction novel. Writers will learn how to make their first pages so intriguing with chapter "hooks" that the reader won't be able to put the book down.

Easy to follow step-by-step instructions on creating a comprehensive plot with the three-act structure using the dynamic templates provided in this guidebook, whether you're a plotter or more of a pantser. Each chapter provides comprehensive tips on storytelling, which every writer needs to plot like an experienced pro without a complicated outline.

Topics in this book include...

* 6 Popular Genre Plot Templates

* *3 Extensive Character Templates*

* *Advice on Writing Scene Hooks*

* *Simple Breakdown on Story Structure*

* *Advice from Bestselling Authors on Plotting*

Also, writers will gain the tools needed to blend character goals within any scene to improve pacing, and instantly strengthen the narrative. Plus, bonus advice on self-publishing and genre word counts. Whether you're writing an intense thriller or a sweeping romance, all novels follow the same basic outline described in detail within this book.

Bestselling author, S. A. Soule also shares her expertise with writers on how to plot a novel quickly through powerful examples in action, along with the necessary tools to immediately deepen the reader's experience.

Are you ready to take your writing skills to the next level?

***

FIRST CHAPTERS

The goal of the first chapter is to create a "tension rope" tight enough to pull the reader into the second, third, and fourth chapters, and on to the end. Your openers in each chapter are very important to keep your reader turning the pages to find out what's going to happen next.

As a freelance editor, I consider it a privilege to edit the work of other aspiring writers. I know each one of them has spent countless hours creating their stories and I love helping them bring out their voice, enrich their prose, and take their writing to the next level. That said, the first chapter is so vital that I work closely with my clients to craft a riveting first paragraph.

The first chapter must be strong and riveting, because the first scene is extremely critical. I really can't overemphasize the importance of getting the first chapter perfect. A writer must captivate the reader in the opening pages or they might lose them altogether.

Every writer should have a firm grasp of basic fiction writing techniques from the first line and paragraph. That is why I repeatedly mention editing overused and abused words.

This next excerpt is the first chapter of my YA novel, RECKLESS REVENGE in the Spellbound series, which is an excellent illustration of how to create suspense, tension, and unanswered questions into your opening pages.

Please examine this example…

Worst part about being a demon hunter was the waiting.

Not paranormals, with their ominous and deadly powers.

Not lycans, with their sharp fangs and unholy yellow stares.

Not even evil witch covens, with their perverse rituals.

Nope. For me it was the waiting that made my job so sucky. My patience was growing thin. I needed to hunt the lycan that murdered my dad—*before* it hunted me.

My fingers clenched the tiger's eye gemstone hanging around my neck on a thin silver chain. Beyond the back fence, giant redwoods soared to heights that seemed to touch the clouds. Cold, inky darkness inched closer to the house, and a tremor slid through my limbs.

At night, most things went to bed. But *scary* things woke up for playtime. Especially living in Fallen Oaks, where they could hide in the habitual fog that drifted over from the San Francisco Bay.

My boyfriend, Trent Donovan—all tall and buffed and smoking hot—and I had been busy making out when branches at the edge of the yard parted and chilling howls pierced the night air. Not coyotes or wolves. This was Northern California. And it wasn't something natural, either. More like a paranormal with a perverse bloodlust.

I held onto Trent's arm, hoping this moment wouldn't be our last.

Can't a girl ever catch a break?

We pulled apart and glanced at each other. Fierce yellow eyes glowed in the darkness.

Now the threat wasn't only hidden within the forest. The newest residents of Fallen Oaks were lycans that must've picked up my scent. Obviously, they'd hunted me down before I could hunt them...

***

I'm beginning the umpteenth revision of one of my novel's openers because I want it to "pop" and grab the reader from the start.

My advice? Try to be impartial, listen to a critique partner's advice, and edit mercilessly—*brutally*! Remember, the goal is to find a literary agent and get published or to create a marketable novel that you can self-publish with pride.

For a first chapter to be successful, it should do at least *one* of the following:

* Appeal to the readers' emotions

* Include unanswered questions

* Hint that something is about to change

* Reveal the main character(s) goal

* Create immediate some type of suspense or dilemma

Don't have your story began with the main characters pondering about their life, or contemplating their present or past situation. If the opening pages introduce something unique about to happen or the overall story problem or hint at the character's goal, but what can (and should) stand in their way of attaining this goal), chances are you have an enticing first chapter. Start at the moment closest to the beginning of the main conflict of your story (inciting incident) as possible.

All first chapters need the following:

Raise some questions

Introduce some stressful conflict

Add suspenseful action

Create a tricky dilemma

Reveal main character(s) goal

Make the reader wonder what is happening, and <u>don't</u> include an explanation.

First chapters should never contain anything slow or stagnant. Just find the first major conflict of the external and internal plot and start in the middle of both. Make sure your first chapter has action, and no lengthy descriptions of settings.

HUMBLE REQUEST

If you read this handbook and find the tools and tips helpful to improving your own storytelling abilities, please consider posting an honest review online.

Word of mouth is crucial for any author's success, and reviews help to spread the book love. So please consider leaving a short *(a sentence or two is fine!)* review wherever you purchased this copy and/or on Good-reads.

If I get enough reviews stating that this guide helped writers to hone their craft, then I'd love to include additional books in this Deep POV series with new topics, such as romance writing, creating suspense, and fictional world-building.

FICTION WRITING TOOLS

Each of these helpful and inexpensive self-editing books in the *Fiction Writing Tools* series encompass many different topics such as, dialogue, exposition, internal-monologue, setting, and other editing techniques that will help creative writers take their writing skills to the next level.

THE WRITER'S GUIDE TO CHARACTER EMOTION

Best Method to Crafting Realistic Character Expressions and Emotions!

Most writers struggle with creating a captivating story. The fastest way to improve your writing is by the use of the "Deep Point-of-View" technique, which can transform any novel from mediocre storytelling into riveting prose.

This manual will provide writers with the essential skills needed to significantly enhance their characterization and intensify emotions by eliminating filtering words that cause narrative distance. Plus, this unique guidebook includes hundreds of amazing ways to use "show don't tell" to submerge readers so deeply into any scene that they will experience the story along with the characters.

Writers will learn to:

* Revise Shallow Writing

* Deepen Characterization

* Craft Realistic Visceral Reactions

* Improve Showing vs. Telling

* Create Lifelike Character Expressions

Bestselling author, S. A. Soule also shares her expertise with writers on how to apply "showing" methods through powerful examples in action, along with the necessary tools to immediately deepen the reader's experience with vivid, sensory details.

THE WRITER'S GUIDE TO CHARACTER EXPRESSIONS

Fastest Way to Improve Dialogue, Settings, and Characterization!

No matter what genre you write, this second manual on the Deep Point of View technique should be kept as a vital reference in every writer's toolbox. This in-depth guide offers specific, practical tools for creative fiction writers on how to craft realistic settings, visceral responses, and lifelike characters.

Crammed with even more examples and ways to eliminate shallow writing, this book provides the necessary techniques to master describing facial expressions, body language, and character emotions. This resource of endless inspiration will reveal how to dig deeper to "show don't tell," which is essential to crafting compelling scenes and deepening characterization.

Learn to write:

* Realistic settings through sensory details

* Three-dimensional characters

* Memorable "Voice"

*Authentic facial expressions

Learn surefire, simple methods of getting readers so emotionally invested in your stories that booklovers will be flipping the pages to find out what happens next.

THE WRITER'S GUIDE TO VIVID SETTINGS AND CHARACTERS

Learn to Describe a Realistic Setting with Atmospheric Detail and Create Vivid Characters!

No matter what genre you write, fiction writers will learn how to craft descriptions like a seasoned pro. World-building isn't easy, but creating original depictions of characters, locations, weather, and mood can greatly enhance anyone's writing.

Evocative settings are more effective and compelling when they're visible, auditory, olfactory, and tactile. And character descriptions are much more visual and lifelike when they have unique physical attributes. This valuable reference and descriptive thesaurus offers writers a simplified way to depict vibrant settings and dynamic character descriptions flawlessly.

Writers will learn:

* The importance of using sensory details

* To expertly master showing vs. telling

* The impact setting can have on a story

* To effectively describe vivid characters

* How adding color will strengthen description

Each chapter provides specific, practical tools to help make writing descriptions and crafting three-dimensional characters simple and fun, with plenty of illustrations to highlight each point.

THE WRITER'S GUIDE TO REALISTIC DIALOGUE

A Powerful Reference Tool to Crafting Realistic Conversations in Fiction!

This manual is specifically for fiction writers who want to learn how to create riveting and compelling dialogue that propels the storyline and reveals character personality.

Writers will also learn how to weave emotion, description, and action into their dialogue heavy scenes. With a special section on how to instantly improve characterization through gripping conversations. All of these helpful writing tools will make your dialogue sparkle!

THE WRITER'S GUIDE TO PLOTTING A NOVEL

Awesome Tips on Crafting a Riveting Story that instantly Grabs Your Reader...

This manual offers amazing techniques for creating stronger beginnings and ways to write a page-turning plot for your fiction novel. Writers will learn how to make their first pages so intriguing with chapter "hooks" that the reader won't be able to put the book down.

Easy to follow step-by-step instructions on creating a comprehensive plot with the three-act structure using the dynamic templates provided in this guidebook, whether you're a plotter or more of a pantser. Each chapter provides comprehensive tips on storytelling, which every writer needs to plot like an experienced pro without a complicated outline.

Topics in this book include:

* 6 Popular Genre Plot Templates

* 3 Extensive Character Templates

* Tools to Create a Page-Turning First Chapter

* Advice on Writing Scene Hooks

* Simple Breakdown on Story Structure

* Wisdom from Bestselling Authors on Plotting

Also, writers will gain the tools needed to blend character goals within any scene to improve pacing, and instantly strengthen the narrative. Plus, bonus advice on self-publishing and genre word counts. Whether you're writing an intense thriller or a sweeping romance, all novels follow the same basic outline described in detail within this book.

THE WRITER'S GUIDE TO AMAZING BOOK BLURBS

An Awesome Book Description is one of the Most Important Tools a Writer Needs to Sell More Books, or to Gain the Attention of an Agent...

Whether you're self-publishing, or querying agents and publishers, this guidebook on book descriptions can help! Writing backjacket copy (blurb or marketing copy) can give most writers a major headache. In this in-depth reference manual, any writer can learn how to instantly create an appealing blurb with a captivating tagline, or write a perfect query letter.

Indie Authors will get a clearer understanding on how to write an effective book description, which is one of the most vital selling points a self-published author needs to successfully promote a book. Book blurbs are a critical marketing tool to attract readers. (Besides a "genre specific" book cover.)

Topics in this book include:

* Book Descriptions: Each chapter offers simple steps to creating powerful blurbs with a gripping opening line, and a strong last sentence "hook."

* Blurb templates: Writers will get 4 simple blurb breakdown templates to learn how to easily write compelling marketing copy.

*Query Letters: If you're a writer, seeking an agent, then crafting an enticing query letter is crucial on the path toward traditional publication. Great cover letters are essential to attracting agents and book publishers.

* Blurb Examples: Over 25 enticing blurbs in almost every genre to unlock your own creativity for self-published novelists.

* Query Templates: Over 10 query letter templates to use for inspiration and guidance for writers striving to get a book publishing contract.

In this valuable resource, there are numerous query letters templates and book blurb examples for almost every fiction genre that will have an agent asking for more, and help a self-published author to write a compelling product description that will boost their book sales.

THE WRITER'S GUIDE TO INDIE BOOK PROMOTION

Learn How To Sell More Books in a Month!

This in-depth marketing guide is perfect for writers publishing their first novel or indie authors trying to gain a wider readership. The manual includes valuable tips on networking, how to get more book reviews, and contains wonderful advice on how to best promote your work from established authors and popular book bloggers.

Whether you're a multi-published author looking to expand your audience or a self-published writer, this book will instantly give you the tools to market your fiction like a pro! Free bonus features include how successful authors use social media to connect with potential readers, reviewers, and how to sell more books.

THE WRITER'S GUIDE TO BOOK COVER SECRETS

An author only has about 5 seconds to lure a reader in with a strong first impression.

Most writers struggle with book promotion and attracting their target readership. In this remarkable guide, indie authors will learn amazing insider tips on book cover design and influential marketing tactics that will increase sales and catch the attention of readers.

A writer works hard on the "inside" of a book, so they should ensure that the "outside" is just as awesome.

Because the secret is…90% of book promotion relies on the "right" cover.

The problem is that most self-published writers are unsure what author branding means or how impactful a genre specific cover is to the effective promotion of a book.

The best way to increase books sales, and save time and money on advertising is by using the secrets revealed in this handbook. The topics included in this in-depth guide also include powerful ways authors of popular genres can attract more readers, along with interviews and advise from some of top designers in the publishing industry.

Utilizing these secrets will help authors connect with readers and widen their audience. If done right, the perfect cover will sell itself and make a massive impact on a book's success.

ABOUT THE AUTHOR

S. A. Soule is a bestselling author and Creativity Coach, who has years of experience working with successful novelists. Many of her fiction and non-fiction books have spent time on the bestseller lists.

Her handbooks in the "Fiction Writing Tools" series are a great resource for writers at any stage in their career, and they each offer helpful advice on how to instantly take your writing skills to the next level and successfully promote your books.

Please feel free to browse her blog, which has some great tips on creative writing online at: *Fiction Writing Tools* and visit her *Creativity Coaching Services* site for help with writing book blurbs, fiction editing, and revising your stories with Deep POV. And don't forget to browse around *SwoonWorthy Book Covers* that has a large selection of designs in every genre.

Made in the USA
San Bernardino, CA
23 May 2020